Andaleeb Wajid is a hybrid author, having published more than forty-five novels in the past fourteen years. Andaleeb enjoys writing in several different genres such as young adult, romance, and horror. Her graphic novel *Scare Walk* (HarperCollins) will be published in 2024. Andaleeb's YA novel *Asmara's Summer*, adapted for a web series, *Dil Dosti Dilemma*, released on Amazon Prime in April 2024.

EVERYTHING SUCKS

ANDALEEB WAJID

Speaking Tiger
YOUNG ADULT

Published by Speaking Tiger Books LLP
125A, Ground Floor, Shahpur Jat,
Near Asiad Village, New Delhi - 110 049

Published in paperback by Speaking Tiger Books in 2024

ISBN: 978-93-5447-850-5
eISBN: 978-93-5447-788-1

10 9 8 7 6 5 4 3 2 1

Typeset in Lora by Jojy Philip
Printed at Chaman Enterprises, New Delhi

1

'What is #GRWM? Is that what you kids are using for the word "grim" these days?'

Kashish looked up from her phone. 'Argh, Api, step away from my laptop please!' she said, snapping her teeth in irritation.

Kinza just waved her off. 'You used to hover by my side ALL the time whenever I was chatting with Kaif,' she said.

Kashish rolled her eyes. 'That was a long time ago. I was *six*. I have no memory of it anyway,' she said, getting up from her bed and walking to the desk where her sister was looking at the Excel sheet open on her laptop. 'Move.'

'You don't have to be rude,' Kinza said huffily. 'It's not like I'm *that* old.'

Kashish wisely kept quiet because of course her sister *was* old. She was almost thirty-five. That was literally a dinosaur. Also, her sister wasn't even like a cool millennial. She was just so out of touch with everything.

'Bol na. What is GRWM?' Kinza insisted, vacating the chair finally.

Kashish sighed. 'It stands for Get Ready With Me.'

Kinza frowned and then looked at the laptop again. 'Wait a minute. Why is this scheduled for every week? And what does that *mean*? You record videos of yourself getting *dressed*?' Her eyes were wide and she looked shocked.

'Why are you here? Don't you usually have something to discuss with Abbu whenever you come to Bangalore?' Kashish deflected.

'Yes, but I also wanted to spend some time with you,' Kinza said, reaching up to pinch her little sister's cheeks like she would do when Kashish was small. Only now, Kashish stepped back, and Kinza frowned.

'Why are you like this?' she asked.

'Why am I like this?' Kashish repeated absently as she sat before her laptop and began checking the items on today's Excel sheet. Her virtual assistant Mili had updated the shared Google sheets calendar for Kashish's Instagram schedule like she did every day.

'Yes. Why have you changed so much?' Kinza asked.

Kashish turned her head and took in her sister who was standing by her desk, hands on her hips.

'Everyone changes,' Kashish said. 'You seem to have forgotten just how much you changed when you got married.'

Drat. She had not planned on throwing that in her sister's face but really, Kinza had some gall telling her that *she* had changed.

Kinza's expression changed rapidly. 'That's old news, isn't it?' she said finally. 'I mean, I got married more than a decade ago.'

Yes. She got married and moved away to be with Kaif in Chennai and then she had two children and then, that was it. Kashish had become an afterthought for her. Kashish couldn't dismiss that bit of her life as old news.

'Anyway, it doesn't matter. I have to shoot a video now, so if you can step out…'

'A video? For your Instagram? I want to see it!' Kinza said, clapping her hands eagerly.

Kashish shook her head. 'No, I can't do it when someone is around,' she said. *Especially you.*

But her sister was adamant. 'You'll need someone to hold the phone, right? Let me do it,' she offered.

'Api, that's not at all needed. Why do you think I have this tripod?'

'Oh. I didn't realise. Let me just hang back in that corner and watch, please?' Kinza said, making a 'please' face at her, one that she couldn't resist.

'Fine. Just stay out of the frame,' Kashish said, walking up to the tripod with the ring light on it.

'And I promise I won't make any noise,' Kinza whispered.

'Yes, don't talk to me and distract me, but it's okay. You don't have to worry about not making any noise. I'll be recording a voiceover for the reel separately,' Kashish explained as she set up the camera.

Kashish didn't see the impressed look her sister was giving her. She was busy setting up the phone and angling it towards her wardrobe, because she would be doing the GRWM post in front of it.

'You do all this by yourself all the time?' Kinza asked in a hushed voice.

'Actually, I have an assistant who does all this for me,' Kashish said. 'But she's got exams right now, so she couldn't come.'

'And you? You don't have any exams?' Kinza asked, sounding very officious and motherly. Kashish merely lifted an eyebrow and didn't bother to reply. Kinza was not her mother.

It took Kashish more than half an hour to shoot the thirty-second reel, where she dressed up in a chic outfit, putting on the layers one by one, followed by the accessories. The edits would take even longer. She wished Mili was around in real-time too. She was so efficient, she would have taken care of all this. But Mili just organised her schedule.

When Kashish looked up, her heart fell the slightest bit. Her sister wasn't there. She hadn't noticed when Kinza had left the room. She must have got bored. Then she heard her outside calling out to her children and something she said gave Kashish pause. She quickly pulled out her diary and jotted it down.

Kinza and the kids were here for the summer holidays. Kashish didn't specially like her niece and nephew much. They ran her sister ragged, making her dance to their tunes.

The door to her room opened softly and Kinza stepped inside, tiptoeing in an exaggerated manner, her finger on her lips. Her children followed her and she made a 'shush' noise, telling them that Kashish aunty was making an important video.

Kashish was editing the clips, making sure they all synced together perfectly. She had lifted the top in her hands and she shook it before the camera and in the next clip, the top was on her. The same with all the other items of clothing and accessories.

'Just Kashish. No need for aunty,' she muttered with a shudder. In college, her friends would laugh at her if they ever heard her being referred to as aunty.

'Okay Just Kashish, show us what you did,' Kinza said, settling on the bed, with the kids around her.

'Just a moment,' Kashish finished stitching the clips together on her phone. She looked up and smiled at the picture they made. Despite her irritation with all three of them, there were times when she could tolerate them just fine.

'I still need to record the voiceover and add the music,' she explained as she walked up to them and sat down on the bed. 'But you can see what it's like without all that.'

Kinza and the kids saw the video with wide eyes. 'Wow,' Kinza said finally. 'How are you so on top of all this stuff?'

Kashish shrugged. 'I have to keep my million followers happy,' she said.

'*Million*?' Kinza shrieked, eyes widening.

Kashish nodded. She had touched a million followers just last month. It had added a new kind of pressure on her, to post all sorts of content, especially the funny stuff.

Kinza handed the phone back to her. 'Just imagine doing all this and becoming famous,' she said. 'In my time, the only reason I was famous was because Kaif and I had consummated our love story on WhatsApp.'

'Eww. TMI, Api!' Kashish said, covering her ears, wondering if the kids needed their ears covered too.

'Chee, no. That's not what I meant. I meant, we *confessed* our love to each other on WhatsApp,' Kinza added quickly.

Shit. She needed to take notes. Would her sister mind if she jotted this down to use in her reels, Kashish wondered.

2

'*I know a lot of people say I'm extraaaaaaa*,' the girl said in a chirpy/screechy voice and Sameer winced, quickly swiping his finger over the screen so that her reel disappeared somewhere into the realms of the Instagram ether. But the next one wasn't any better.

He turned to his younger brother Sadeem who was lounging on his bed in their shared bedroom, his eyes fixed on his own phone.

'Why are you making me look at this again?' he asked, flinging his phone on the bed and getting up to stretch.

'Because you need to know what everyone else is doing,' Sadeem retorted without even looking up.

'Why? *My* stuff is good,' Sameer said.

'Says you.'

'No, says the number of views my reel got,' Sameer said.

Sadeem sat up and made a scoffing noise in his throat. 'That was a fluke. And it was ONE reel. And I think we got those views because you accidentally showed them that you're buff.'

Sameer frowned. 'Making these reels is a total waste of my time' he said, scratching his head absently.

'Who was it who said that this account can be a repository of family recipes?' Sadeem asked, narrowing his eyes.

Sameer sighed. It had all started when he was visiting Ammajan, his grandmother, in Vellore with Sadeem, and he told her how much he missed her chicken Chettinad. She had slapped him lightly and said that once she was gone, who would make it for him?

'Don't say all that Ammajan!' he had said, but it got him thinking. He wanted to have a repository of recipes, especially whatever food Ammajan cooked. And he didn't just want written recipes. He wanted to cook it with her. So he had asked Sadeem to record a video of them making it.

He hadn't known that his wily brother had edited the video and uploaded it to Sameer's Instagram and YouTube, and for some reason, it had blown up.

'I know I said that, but doing all this along with college work is such a pain!'

Sadeem, who was in class 11, stood up and cleared his throat. 'This is why you should hire me as your social media manager,' he said, with a flourish and a bow.

Sameer stared at him and then laughed.

'I'm serious, bro!' Sadeem said, looking offended.

'Err…what will you even do?' Sameer asked.

'Your Instagram page is on the verge of 10k followers. You just need to post a little more regularly, and nudge the others into following you.'

'But how?'

'That is why you need to do some research and see what everyone else is putting out there,' Sadeem informed him.

'If you're my social media manager, will you do it?' Sameer asked.

Sadeem straightened his back even further. 'Of course. I mean, you're giving me a *legit* reason to check out Instagram and get *paid* for it? I'd be mad not to!'

'Paid?' Sameer asked with a frown.

'You seriously don't expect me to work for free, do you?' Sadeem asked, lifting an eyebrow.

'Okay, what exactly will you be doing as my "social media manager"?' Sameer asked, making air quotes with his fingers.

Sadeem opened his mouth to explain something when the door was pushed open by Ammi who peered inside.

'Even on Sundays I have to call you both to come and eat lunch?' she asked irritably.

Sadeem expelled a breath and then stretched out his arms. 'Ammi, matashree, mothership…you are never at home on any other day to give us lunch,' he said, making Sameer snicker.

Ammi just rolled her eyes. 'Come now before the food gets cold,' she said, shaking her head at him and walking away.

'Say no more! Mutton phaal, here I come!' Sadeem started marching towards the door when Sameer stopped him.

'You know what? *You* should be the one doing these reels. You're funny and quirky and from what I see, that sort of stuff really works,' he said. He could never be funny.

‘Funny is a dime a dozen. The world needs more hot nerds like you,’ Sadeem quipped. ‘Keep doing your thing. I’ll help you boost those numbers.’

They both walked outside where Abbu was waiting at the dining table, reading the newspaper. ‘Have you been reading the paper since morning?’ Sameer asked.

‘Your father hasn’t moved from there at all since breakfast,’ Ammi complained as she sat down at the dining table. Abbu peered at them from the top of the paper and put it away with a sigh.

Much later, after lunch was done and they’d all tucked into bowls of ice cream for dessert, Sadeem started again.

‘Gave it some thought?’ he asked.

‘You really have no idea how to work with your pocket money every month, right? That’s why you want me to pay you for your help,’ Sameer said.

Sadeem shrugged. ‘School’s expensive, bro,’ he said.

‘For what? You’re not paying your own fees,’ Sameer scoffed. At the mention of the word ‘fees’, Abbu’s ears pricked up and he tried to tune into them but got bored soon after and dozed off.

‘What do you even know about the life of a class 11 student?’ Sadeem said dramatically.

‘I was literally there two years ago,’ Sameer reminded him, slapping the top of Sadeem’s head lightly. Of course Ammi had to see that and she glared at him.

‘No hitting on the head!’ she admonished. ‘Haven’t I told you a hundred times?’

More like a million times, Sameer thought. ‘But I can hit him anywhere else then?’ he asked.

Ammi made a face. 'Why are you two hitting each other?' she asked.

Sadeem rubbed the top of his head. 'Nothing, you go back to what you were doing,' he told Ammi who glared at him now.

'All week I have to listen to men tell me what I have to do. Don't you dare start it at home,' she warned.

The boys decided it was best to keep quiet. Ammi worked at a bank and she did not appreciate being reminded that she was not the boss there. Yet.

After a moment, Sameer slid down from the sofa to the floor and turned to Sadeem. 'Why exactly do we need to grow my numbers?'

Sadeem looked excited that he was considering it. 'I know you didn't dream of becoming an Instagram influencer. But think of the benefits. Think of the fun. Think of the girls!' he added the last with a wink.

Sameer blushed. If only he had half of his brother's flirting capacity. But the idea excited him and he enjoyed checking Instagram to see comments from people who had seen that viral video of him cooking with Ammajan.

'Okay, I'll take you up on your offer,' Sameer said.

Sadeem extended his hand solemnly and after staring at it for a few seconds, Sameer shook it. Ammi was looking at both of them sceptically.

'Whatever. Don't even tell me what you guys are up to,' she muttered as she changed channels on the TV. A song blared out and Abbu woke from his nap with a jump.

3

The dining table at Kashish's home that night was in a mess. It was covered with crayons and sheets of paper and two very busy children were colouring everything except the paper. Kinza was cooking dinner in the kitchen, calling out instructions every now and then to them, which they ignored.

When Kashish stepped outside her room, she surveyed the scene stoically. The crayon marks could be wiped away but the diligent way in which Kabir was digging the crayon into the table itself, meant it would most certainly leave behind more than a trace of its existence.

She glanced at Abbu who was watching the news on the TV. The only indication that he was being affected by the two children was in the way the volume of the TV increased slowly but surely.

'Didn't Akka cook dinner for us?' Kashish asked Abbu as she lowered herself into the sofa next to him.

'She did,' Abbu replied. Then he nodded in the general direction of the kids and Kinza. 'Madam here and her kids refused to eat it. So she decided to cook.'

Kashish didn't say anything. She loved Kinza's cooking but had had to do without it for so long that she didn't want to get used to it again. Resentment simmered inside her as she folded her arms across her chest.

'You should go and see if she needs any help,' Abbu said.

Kashish stared at him. He couldn't possibly be serious.

'Go and see what she's doing,' Abbu urged her.

Gritting her teeth, Kashish got up and walked to the kitchen. What she saw there made her pause for a moment. Kinza was intently watching a video on her phone.

'You're not cooking?' she asked. Kinza looked up briefly and smiled.

'I am! I'm just looking up this recipe on YouTube,' she said.

Kinza was on YouTube? But of course. She watched all her Pakistani TV shows on it.

'See this boy? He's so cute,' she said, almost blushing. Kashish peered down at the screen.

He *was* cute. And so very sincere.

'You're following a recipe he's showing?' Kashish asked, surprised. Kinza nodded but didn't elaborate.

Kashish watched as the boy on the screen continued to stir something in a pot.

'What's he making?' she asked when Kinza didn't move.

'Chicken Chettinad,' Kinza replied. Then she swiped across the screen and put the phone down.

'And you're making that too?'

'Oh no, I'm making paneer butter masala,' she said.

'What?'

Kinza nodded. 'I was just waiting for the tomato-onion mixture to cool down before blending it. How come you're here?'

'Abbu said I should see if you need any help,' Kashish said sullenly.

'No, it's under control. Or maybe you can just knead the dough for the chapatis?' Kinza asked.

Ugh. She hated doing that. All the dough got stuck to her fingernails and it took forever to remove it.

'Didn't Akka make chapatis?' she asked, stalling.

Kinza made a face. 'How do you guys even eat that? It's like rubber. And that kurma she made…' She shuddered.

And now, Kinza would get them used to her soft-as-butter chapatis and once she left, they would have to go back to eating the rubbery ones that Akka made for them with the disgusting kurma. Just great.

With a mutinous look on her face, Kashish measured out the atta in a bowl while Kinza transferred the tomato and onion mixture to a mixer-grinder.

'This is nice,' Kinza said, as she plugged it into the wall outlet.

'What?' Kashish asked, watching with dismay because she'd put too much water in the atta and was now looking at a watery mess.

'You and me, in the kitchen together after so long. You were always so busy whenever I came all these years with your school and Boards and all that,' Kinza said.

Kashish didn't respond to that. What could she say after all?

'And I think it helps that you're doing a Humanities course in college. Must be fun,' Kinza said with a sigh.

'Fun it isn't, but it's relatively less pressure,' Kashish tried to add more atta to compensate for the extra water.

'Pch. What have you done?' Kinza said, glancing at the bowl. 'You leave it. I'll fix it.'

Gladly, Kashish thought as she tried to get rid of the sticky dough on her fingers at the sink.

'So what are your plans after this?' Kinza asked.

'I'm going to post a few stories and then…'

'No, I meant after college,' Kinza interrupted her but she switched on the mixer-grinder to blitz the tomato and onion mixture and no one could hear anything over the whirr.

Kashish wasn't sure what she was expected to say. But the pause gave her time to collect her thoughts. What *did* she want to do? She was making quite a bit of money through Instagram collaborations and paid promotions. But could she do this for the rest of her life? The thought was not very reassuring.

When Kinza switched off the mixer, she looked at Kashish. 'Now tell,' she said.

Why? Why was Kinza showing all this interest in her? Just so she could forget about her when she went back to Chennai at the end of the week?

'I don't know yet,' Kashish said.

Kinza looked at her for a moment too long. 'That's okay,' she said. 'Not knowing what to do with your life is something that stays the same for all generations, apparently.'

Kashish didn't ask what Kinza meant. She and her sister didn't share that sort of an equation any longer. She wiped her hands on the towel and walked away from there.

4

There was a time when Kinza would be there for Kashish from the moment she opened her eyes in the morning. If baby Kashish squeaked, Kinza would pick her up, coo to her softly, give her a bottle. For the longest time, Kashish used to think she had two mothers. And she used to secretly think that Kinza was the better mother than Ammi.

Ammi was wonderful, yes, but she was also easily tired and didn't have the energy for her. Ammi hadn't been keeping well after Kashish was born. She'd had her when she was almost forty, and fallen sick soon thereafter. Moreover, Kashish could cuddle with Kinza in a way she never could with Ammi. The two of them would sit together and watch wholly unsuitable shows like *Desperate Housewives* because that was what Kinza wanted to watch.

When Kashish was around five, Kinza was often quite distracted and didn't want to hang out with her like she used to. Kinza was twenty-one and had just met Kaif. She often came back home from college, her eyes glittering and Kashish thought she hadn't seen anyone more beautiful than her older sister.

Apparently, Kaif thought so too. But the two of them wanted to wait until she finished her post-graduation and he was settled in his job as well. So for around four years, Kashish observed her sister sneaking around to talk in whispers to Kaif on her phone, and sometimes, she'd be around during their video calls as well, where they wouldn't really say anything but just stare at each other.

When Kinza finally got married, Kashish was confused because she couldn't understand why everyone was crying after the nikah. When it sank in finally that Kinza wouldn't be living with them any more, Kashish started bawling. Ammi had to hold her tightly to stop her from running after Kinza's car.

But that wasn't the worst of it.

A few months after their marriage, Kinza and Kaif came home and told Ammi and Abbu that they were moving to Chennai.

That was the first time Kashish knew heartbreak. At least, she thought it was the worst thing in the world, but then the following year…Ammi…

Kashish sat up in bed and wiped her face, annoyed at finding it wet. Had she been crying in her sleep? She found that hard to believe. She reached out and flicked on the switch of her table lamp and pulled out a few tissues from a box.

Last night, after dinner, they had watched Kinza and Kaif's wedding video. Both her kids were oohing and aahing about how glamorous their mother looked when Kabir started crying because he wasn't in the video. Kashish was annoyed as the brats kept pointing to her whenever she appeared on the screen, and okay, she'd been nine or ten, and her hairstyle was dumb. But they kept laughing at it, and Kashish fast forwarded to all the bits with Ammi in it.

She didn't know which hurt more—Kinza's defection or Ammi's loss. They were both tied in her mind together, irrevocably. She still grieved for her mother and the walls she built in her heart let no one in—especially not her sister.

Kashish glanced at the clock. It was past one. She had a nine a.m. class and needed to sleep. She didn't want to be late. She'd heard enough disparaging comments from Sr Amelia that even celebrity influencers needed to get their degrees.

But sleep eluded her. She looked around her room, at the corner where she shot her videos, and for the first time, she didn't feel any sort of jolt inside. She wondered how someone else would have mined this for content.

What to do when you wake up in the middle of the night, crying for the mother you lost at ten?

Um, no.

She couldn't put herself out there like that for the world to see. She could never understand how people cried on camera—not actors, but normal people like her. How did they post videos of themselves after breakups or after getting yelled at by someone.

Some part of her would always be closed. She couldn't share that with the world. Everything else was there for the taking—her life, her ambitions, her vlogs, her funny videos, but the true essence of who she was could never go out into the world.

Never.

She grabbed her phone from the bedside table and opened Instagram and started scrolling through it out of sheer boredom.

Wait. That was the cute guy whose video Kinza had been looking at earlier while cooking. Her finger hovered uncertainly and she tapped open the video to see it.

In the video, he was not talking, dancing, or acting. He was kneading atta with a grim expression on his face, wearing a tight grey T-shirt that outlined his biceps. He looked up once at the camera, and Kashish drew in a breath.

It felt like he was looking at her.

Caramel brown eyes piercing into her very soul.

Her mouth dropped open and her eyes fell to the likes going up, with hearts floating away. She had no clue what he was making, but her eyes watched the way his biceps flexed as he kneaded the dough. He pulled and stretched it on the counter, and Kashish's mouth turned dry.

Whatever he was doing, she wanted him to keep doing it.

And then she blinked and let out a groan. Oh god. How could she have fallen for this? Here was one more guy, trying to look sexy in the kitchen. Ugh. She hated all the Cedrik Lorenzen wannabes because a) there couldn't be another Cedrik and b) he made it look effortlessly sexy while everyone else looked like they were trying too hard.

'Gross!' she muttered angrily and scrolled away, but something made her come back to the video once more.

She watched as he kneaded the dough and then, again he did that thing, looking into the camera. She watched right till the end when he rolled out the rotis on a tawa, lifting one eyebrow invitingly.

For some reason, she was just annoyed by this Sameer Ehsan. Annoyed at the way his biceps popped when he rolled out the roti. But she was more irritated with the number of likes his video was garnering.

She didn't know why, but she was going to do something about it.

5

'I won't do it again. I'm sorry.'

Sadeem looked anything but sorry as he gave his older brother an ingratiating smile.

'I told you I wasn't comfortable with all that, Sadeem!' Sameer barked when he saw the sort of comments his latest reel was getting.

Sadeem had insisted that he not talk, but just broodingly look at the camera now and then. He said it went with his image of the hot nerd and he was sure that his follower count would jump drastically. Sameer hadn't been even one bit convinced. And he wasn't comfortable with it. But Sadeem kept telling him how the earlier video had got so many likes and he would be just a flash in the pan if he didn't keep up.

Sadeem winced. 'But look at it this way. You've now got 20k followers. And it's growing. A *simple* video of you kneading atta and making roti has some twenty-five thousand likes.'

Sameer put his phone face down on the bedside table and covered his eyes with his forearm. 'I wish I hadn't listened to you,' he muttered.

Sadeem, who was sitting on a stool between the two beds, pulled the stool closer to his brother. 'I know you feel like this is objectifying you, but why can't we make use of what we've got bro?'

'Which is?' Sameer asked, lowering his arm, and looking down at him.

'You're hot. Did you see the comments you got from girls? Women?'

Sameer blushed instantly. He did not want to recall the number of peach, fire, and panting emojis the reel had received. He was shy and this new-found fame didn't sit well with him.

Sadeem went on in a hurry. 'Look, you don't have to do a single thing about those comments. Let it be. We have to work on the next video. And we have to look at a way of setting ourselves apart. You cannot just be another hot guy in the kitchen trying to make cooking look like sex.'

Sameer stared at his younger brother for a few moments. No tell-tale blush on his face at all.

'So I shouldn't wear my two-size small T-shirt in the kitchen again, right?' he asked.

'Oh no. I'm getting you sleeveless T-shirts for the videos,' Sadeem replied nonchalantly.

'Didn't you just tell me you won't do it again?' Sameer asked, sitting up on his bed and staring at his brother mutinously.

'That was just to appease you. I'm trying to make you see sense,' Sadeem countered.

'What did you mean we have to look at a way of setting ourselves apart?' Sameer asked, his hand automatically straying to his phone because now he was addicted to checking the number of views the video had received. Each like and comment was a rush, one he hadn't anticipated he'd enjoy so much, despite the hard time he was giving his brother.

'I'm thinking. I'm thinking. Listen, these videos have to lead to the YouTube channel because that's serious stuff right there once we get a decent number of subscribers.'

Sameer shrugged. He had set up the YouTube channel some months ago and posted there sporadically. The video with Ammajan had made him popular though and he knew Sadeem was right. It was time to revive the channel.

'What are you doing?' Sameer asked, narrowing his eyes.

'Reading your DMs,' Sadeem said nonchalantly.

'WHAT?' Sameer roared. He pounced on his younger brother but Sadeem was quicker and he darted away.

'Hey! I'm your social media manager. Do you really think celebs read their own DMs?' he asked, scoffing as he held his phone away.

Sameer paused in the middle of trying to snatch away his phone.

'When did you add my account to your phone?' he asked, his jaw tight.

'Just before posting the new video. Come on. It makes sense for me to have the account on my phone too. I can do a lot of promotion if I have easy access to your account.' Sadeem had a point but still…it felt like everything was rapidly flying away out of Sameer's control.

'Fine. But leave my DMs alone!' Sameer said, sitting back on the bed. He felt a little tug in his belly when he saw that his video had reached an added 1000 or so likes in the time they'd been arguing.

Sadeem put his hands up. 'Yes, okay fine. I thought I'd weed out all the crap for you but I get it. You don't want me to hover over your private messages.'

Sameer stared at his brother for a few moments. Then, the two of them went back to their own phones. Outside, he could hear the comforting sound of the TV and the muted murmur of their parents talking. It was a week night and right on cue, at ten, Ammi pushed open the door and stared down at them both.

'It's a week night. Lights out and go to sleep both of you,' she said crisply.

'Aye, aye, captain!' Sadeem said with a salute.

Ammi sighed and rolled her eyes. 'What did I do to get this joker for a son…'

'You wound me,' Sadeem said, clutching his chest dramatically.

'Your heart is on the other side,' Sameer said, unable to stop smiling at his brother's antics. Sadeem switched his hand to the other side swiftly, making it look even funnier. Sameer saw his mother fighting hard not to smile.

'Idiot,' she muttered affectionately. As she closed the door, she pointed at the lights. 'Off,' she mouthed.

Sameer got up and switched off the lights, then fumbled back to his bed in the eerie blue night light.

'I was thinking, big bro…' Sadeem started.

Sameer stared at the fluorescent, plastic stars that he and Sadeem had stuck on the ceiling eons ago. They glowed weakly and he blinked.

'Your video with Ammajan was the starting point for all this, right?' Sadeem went on.

'Yeah, but you know that video took forever to shoot. It's not easy getting her to listen to instructions,' Sameer reminded his brother, a fond smile on his face. 'And she's not easily accessible. We don't travel to Vellore that often in any case.'

'True. But what if…what if we shot a few reaction snippets of her saying her trademark things. Like when she calls you "nalayakh potta" and…'

'Excuse me, she calls *you* that. Not me,' Sameer said indignantly. 'But what are you thinking?'

Sadeem was silent for so long, Sameer thought he'd fallen asleep.

'I know what we're going to do!' he said, sitting up and rubbing his hands with glee.

'Shush! Keep it down or Ammi …'

Once again, Ammi opened the door to their room. 'Do I even want to know what's going on?' she asked.

Sameer was tempted to tell her that they were no longer adolescents but young men now. They often stayed up until the wee hours of the morning watching football and wrestling matches and she never found out. Sure, they dozed a bit in classes the following day, but that was all right. And she couldn't treat them like they were ten and twelve. But he valued his life, so he kept quiet. They pretended to sleep, and with a sigh, she shut the door with a click.

'Don't,' Sameer warned him softly. 'We'll talk tomorrow.'

6

Kashish returned from college exhausted. She was dreading being back home because Kinza was leaving the following morning. It was going to be her last night with her sister and she had no idea when she would see her again.

She would, however, not miss these brats, she thought as she skidded on a banana peel in the living room and managed to miraculously stay upright. Gritting her teeth, she stomped into her bedroom and found the two brats seated at *her* desk, flipping through *her* diary, and oh-my-god-this-cant-be-happening, Kabir was scribbling on her diary with a fat crayon.

Both kids looked startled when they saw her and Kabir dropped the crayon immediately. But then, he picked it up and went back to what he was doing. Kainaat stared at her anxiously. She had been brushing her hair with *her* hairbrush. Long, silky strands of her hair lay in a pool on the desk where she was seated, supervising her brother ruin Kashish's diary.

This was it. She couldn't take it any longer.

Breathe in. Breathe out. Control yourself.

That schedule took a week to set up and now…

It's okay. They're gone tomorrow morning. Her life would go back to normal.

But what about all this mess?

Even as she was screaming at the kids in her mind, a part of her was noting down everything for a future video she could make out of it. But a temper outburst was imminent.

She swivelled on her feet and walked outside, swiftly typing out a text to Rania, telling her that she was on her way over.

Rania replied instantly—*What happened?*

Sighing, Kashish started typing back when she walked smack into Kinza who had been looking for her kids.

'Hey! You're back? Did you see where the kids are?' she asked.

They're in my room, scribbling all over my events diary and making a mess of my desk and my life.

Kashish didn't say the words she really wanted to, but gave her sister a tight smile. 'I'm going to Rania's house. I'll be back later.'

'No, no, wait! I want to talk to you,' Kinza said, tugging her arm and leading her back inside her bedroom where she stopped short on seeing her kids.

'Kabir! No! You can't write on that and what are you doing Kainaat!' Kinza yelled, loud enough to startle even Kashish.

Both kids looked up guiltily. 'Sorry, Just Kashish Aunty,' Kainaat said, but she didn't look even a little bit sorry. She dropped the tube of lipstick that she'd been using to daub over her lips.

Kashish was calculating how long it would take for her to get over her mental trauma of seeing all her precious things being so casually destroyed. 'I have to go meet Rania now. Can't this wait?' Something in the middle of her chest pinched and she breathed through it.

Kinza turned to her and gave her the same glare she was giving her children. 'No, it can't. And didn't you just meet Rania in college? Unless meeting her is code for meeting some boy and…'

'Oh god, no. I need some space,' Kashish burst out angrily. 'I'll see you tonight.'

'Kashish, wait. I wanted to ask you to come and stay at my place for a few days,' Kinza said quickly. Kashish paused and turned around.

'What?'

Kinza nodded. 'Why are you so surprised? I call you every year and each time you make some excuse, about Board exams and this and that. But now you don't have to worry about all that. Come and stay with me after your semester exams.'

Kashish didn't even think before speaking. 'But why?'

'Why? Because you're my little sister and I want to spend time with you,' Kinza remarked, as if it was obvious.

'And Kaif Bhai is okay with it?' she asked finally. Her voice felt rusty.

Kinza frowned. 'Why on earth would he not be okay with it?' she asked incredulously.

There were a number of things that Kashish wanted to tell her sister. But the primary one was that she felt this overture was too little, too late. But perhaps she was being unfair. As she'd mentioned, Kinza had kept inviting her, but Kashish never went to Chennai to stay with her.

'I'll think about it,' she said, and then turned around to leave.

'You're sure there's no boy?' Kinza called out as Kashish left.

Kashish rolled her eyes. 'As if I'd tell you if there was,' she muttered.

'I heard that!' Kinza called back. 'And come back soon for dinner. I'm making kacchi biryani.'

Kashish's mouth trembled and in her internal war over her anger and hunger, the latter won. Instead of going to Rania's house as she had planned, she turned right back around and walked into her room. She needed a shower. She needed some mental space.

Her sister had invited her to stay with her. Her sister was leaving tomorrow. She would tolerate the brats to spend this last evening with her, or she knew she'd regret it. And her sister was making her famed kacchi biryani.

'Fine. I'm not going out. But I need you all to leave my room because I need a shower,' she said.

'I was just going to tell you why on earth are you going to this Rania's house without showering,' Kinza said with narrowed eyes.

Kashish rolled her eyes once more. Her sister whispered as she walked past her. 'Your deo is clearly not working, Munni. You stink.'

Kashish's mouth dropped open. And unfortunately, Kinza's kids had her sharp hearing. 'Munni stinks! Munni stinks!' they prattled.

She shut the door on their faces, and turned around. Something was surely up. Kinza hadn't called her Munni in years. But the invitation was genuine and maybe this time, she would take her up on it.

Her phone beeped. It was a message from Rania. A single question mark.

Her fingers flew over the screen as she told her friend she'd meet her in college the next day and tell her everything.

7

After much discussion between the brothers, it was decided that they would go to Vellore during the weekend and convince Ammajan to come and stay with them for a few days. Ammi scoffed at their plans.

'She's never going to come with you two. And she's never going to agree to stay here,' she said, as she packed their dabbas for lunch efficiently, before moving on to packing hers and Abbu's as well.

'Why not? We're her favourite grandchildren,' Sameer said with a frown.

'Only the eldest ones are her favourite,' Ammi reminded them. 'That's why she likes you more. Just like she likes Fiza more than Basit.' Ammi's brother Naim uncle lived in Chennai, and when they were younger, summer vacations to Vellore often meant they would all travel together. But things had changed since they all grew up and their holidays never synced for them to travel at the same time.

'Well, since I'm clearly her favourite, she might listen,' Sameer said. Sadeem scowled but said nothing.

'You might have a chance at this if you gang up with Fiza and tell her to invite Ammi too. You know she always prefers to stay in Naim's house than ours,' Ammi remarked.

'And that's so annoying!' Sadeem burst out finally.

'That's her son's house. This is her daughter's,' Ammi said with a practical shrug as she zipped the lunch box in the bag she took to work. 'I don't want to push her or make her uncomfortable.'

Sameer didn't like the way his mother was so cool and accepting about the status quo. 'So there's some rule that she can't stay at her daughter's home but she can at her son's?'

Ammi shook her head. 'No rules as such,' she said, looking over her shoulder. 'Society. Expectations.'

Sadeem made a puke-y face which thankfully for him, Ammi didn't see. Ammi now remembered something else.

'Hey. There's one way you can get her to come to Chennai and stay for a few days and she might even agree to stay here.'

'How? She's not going to jump on board because we need her for my Instagram reels,' Sameer muttered.

Ammi rolled her eyes at that. 'No, but there's a wedding happening next month. Nothing will make her leave Vellore faster than a wedding,' she said.

Sameer groaned. 'Whose wedding?' he asked.

'One of Fiza's cousins.'

'Must be on Mami's side,' Sameer remarked.

'Obviously. But we'll be invited too, and she might agree to stay here because it can get chaotic in Naim's house and she won't want to be in the way,' Ammi said with a lot of self-assurance.

'Ugh. I hate weddings,' Sameer said, making a sulking face. Ammi gave him a fake-sweet smile that did not bode well for him. He wondered if she expected both of them to wear pathanis in the Chennai heat.

When Ammi left, Sadeem turned to him. He was dressed in his school uniform and he looked nothing like the prankster he normally was.

'A wedding is going to be a HUGE chance for you to find content for Instagram!' he said, excitement gleaming in his eyes.

'Eh. My reels are about cooking. And we wanted Ammajan to record some while she's here in the *kitchen*. With *me*. Not at some wedding.'

'Don't worry, bro. Your social media manager will figure out something. Speaking of,' he mumbled through a mouthful of idli as he sat at the kitchen island and ate. He pulled out his phone and opened Instagram.

'What the f…' Sadeem muttered loudly before trailing away, realising that Ammi might still be in the house and might not take kindly to hear an expletive leave his mouth.

'What?' Sameer asked, blinking. His brother looked furious.

'See this.'

Sameer took the phone from him and stared at the reel of him kneading atta. 'This is my reel, so why…' He stopped talking because he realised that someone had remixed his reel and the moment his clip ended, it showed a girl, dressed like he had been, with fake stubble on her chin and cheeks doing everything he had been doing, but in an exaggerated way. Even the way he looked into the camera. She was wearing a cap backwards and her over-the-top expressions were almost funny, until he remembered that she was mocking him.

A caption played out at the bottom of the screen as she realised her hands were covered with sticky dough—*When you try too hard, things get messy.*

This ended with a close-up of her sticky atta-covered hand, but edited to make it look like she'd covered his face with it.

'What the hell is this?' he asked, sitting down at the island.

Sadeem yelped when he checked the time on the wall clock. 'I'm getting late for school. I can't use the phone there. But you need to…' he frowned as he saw something on the screen. 'Maybe this is a good thing. I'll come back and take care of it,' he said as he picked up his school bag and rushed outside.

Sameer chewed his lips. He didn't like this. His stomach clamped and clenched and he instantly felt foolish. He knew no one enjoyed being mocked at. But this hit him hard. He had done something out of his comfort zone and for no rhyme or reason, some stranger had made fun of him, and put it up for her…one million followers to see.

His face turned hot. Then he did the one thing he should not have done. He went down the rabbit hole of Kashish Asif's Instagram page.

8

Kashish was sitting in Rania's aqua and white colour-coordinated bedroom, staring into space, thinking about how empty the house would feel once she went back home. Abbu would be back from office but that didn't make much of a difference. He would sit in his corner of the living room, while she sat in her room, until they both went to the dining table to quietly eat whatever awful food Akka had prepared for them.

She hadn't gone home after college, needing a little time for herself to mentally prepare for the loneliness that would inevitably strike her. Last night, she'd actually managed to overlook the bratty behaviour of Kinza's kids, and allowed herself to have fun, even though deep inside, she was worried about how she would deal with their absence.

'Why are you so tense?' Rania asked, as she brought in a tray of snacks sent by her mother.

'Nothing really,' Kashish said. She was close to Rania, but she didn't want to see that flare of pity in her best friend's eyes when she told her about the loneliness and how it got to her sometimes. It got worse whenever Kinza left and her best defence against it was by not opening up. Last night, the lure of kacchi biryani had kept her at home and now she was regretting it.

'Well, the new video has got loads of comments,' Rania said.

'As expected,' Kashish said, momentarily forgetting her woes and thinking about the vicious stab of joy she'd felt when she'd uploaded the video finally. For a moment, she'd held back, asking herself why she was doing this. That boy had done nothing to her. He was a stranger on the internet. And she wasn't on Instagram to pick fights with strangers. But that's what she'd done. She'd poked a bear, even if he had a measly twenty thousand followers. And she needn't have.

'You were a bitch to him, bro,' Rania said, picking up a samosa and crunching through it, offering one to Kashish with her other hand.

Kashish winced as she picked up the samosa.

'I know.'

'And it's not like he deserved it,' Rania went on.

'Listen, I know that. But it's Instagram. This sort of stuff is here today, gone tomorrow and maybe it will get him more followers. I might have done him a favour,' Kashish protested. She didn't want Rania to make her feel extra shitty. The little burst of pleasure she'd felt had dissipated long ago and it was hard to hold on to it. She couldn't quite explain to anyone why she'd felt the need to pull Sameer Ehsan down a peg or two. She just wanted to do something in that moment, and she'd done it.

'Um, my mother says the internet remembers everything. You can't put something out there and undo it,' Rania said, her eyebrows going up as she saw something on her phone.

Kashish ignored her for a moment as she ate the samosa. The kheema filling was juicy and delicious and she wasn't really in the mood to remind Rania to keep her opinions to herself. She knew how the internet worked, thank you very much, even if she didn't have a mother to remind her about it.

'What are you looking at?' she asked, when Rania continued to stare at her phone, open-mouthed. A nervous giggle escaped and she looked up at Kashish, a look of confusion mingled with delight on her face.

'What happened?' Kashish asked. 'Is it a message from…'

'Shush! Don't say his name here!' Rania said, looking around apprehensively. Kashish rolled her eyes.

'Fine. Your boyfriend?' Kashish whispered and Rania slapped her own forehead.

'This isn't about him,' she whispered back. Then, in a louder voice, she cleared her throat. 'See for yourself.'

Kashish took the proffered phone.

It was that boy, Sameer. He had remixed her remix, and recorded a new video after hers, where he'd done some terrible editing to put her face on the ball of atta that he slapped on the counter. Repeatedly.

Kashish covered her mouth with her hand. It was hilarious. Especially because he looked so serious while he was doing it.

'Why did he do this?' she asked, chortling.

'You're not mad?' Rania asked her, finally giggling.

'No, I'm not. I'm just...' Kashish didn't know what to say. She felt challenged, somehow. And that was a far cry from the feelings of desolation and loneliness that had crept up on her. She grabbed on to it with both hands and felt a burst of exhilaration travel through her insides.

The video ended with him slapping the ball of dough on the counter so hard, that it split into multiple balls, each with her face floating on it.

'Oh my god, this is like one of those 90s wedding videos!' Rania shrieked, laughing out loud. 'My parents' wedding video is exactly like this!'

'Their faces are on atta and they're being smacked around?' Kashish asked.

Rania shook her head but the two of them were laughing uncontrollably now.

'Did you read the caption?' Kashish asked, holding on to her stomach now.

'No, what does it say? That you're Atta Kashish?'

'No, see,' Kashish said, wiping at the tears from her eyes. 'Sometimes you need to beat atta to make it soft and stretchy and pliable. Sometimes you need to beat it harder,' Kashish read out.

'Huh,' Rania stopped laughing. She shook her head. 'That's not funny.'

'Yeah. He shouldn't have included the caption.' The mirth disappeared from Kashish's eyes. 'It's like promoting domestic violence.'

'It is,' Rania agreed.

They were both silent, as the reel played again. It didn't seem that funny now.

'What are you going to do about it?' Rania asked finally.

She had to respond. She'd started this. She didn't mind her face on the atta, but she had to do something about the caption and what he seemed to imply. And in that context, her face on the atta was not a good idea at all.

She looked at his serious face, at those caramel brown eyes that had caught her attention the first time she saw him, and wished once more that she'd never remixed his reel. But she couldn't stay quiet now. His reel was promoting something dangerous.

'Have to take him down,' she said quietly.

'Maybe send him a DM and tell him to take down his video? Because of what it seems to imply?' Rania suggested.

Kashish contemplated it for a moment and then she shook her head. 'Nah. He should have better sense than that.'

Rania didn't say anything but Kashish knew what she had to do.

9

'You did not.'

'I did.'

Sameer and Sadeem stared at each other.

'I told you I'll come home and take care of it,' Sadeem fumed.

'I know. But I just had to do something,' Sameer said. His gut twisted and churned. He felt foolish and stupid for the video he'd posted earlier that day.

'But that?' Sadeem asked, his mouth dropping open. 'That's insane.'

'I *know*,' Sameer said, with a groan. He sat down on the dining table chair, covering his forehead with his hands. 'I should have thought it through. I was just trying to mock her and…'

'And you ended up saying *that*? Beat harder? Not funny, bro,' Sadeem said, rubbing his cheek with agitation.

'I don't know why it sounded funny to me in that moment. I just went with it,' Sameer admitted. He'd stayed home from college, worked all day on making that ridiculous video, and an hour after he posted it, he realised exactly what he'd done.

By then it was too late. The reel had been shared and re-shared, mostly by men who were having a laugh at his and Kashish's expense, and according to Sadeem, he had a bunch of new followers who were most likely incels. He had deleted the reel and now he needed to post an apology video.

'How could you think putting her face on the atta was funny?' Sadeem asked. 'And how did you even do that?'

Sameer didn't bother replying. He was feeling too miserable as it was. What had he been thinking? He hadn't been thinking, clearly. But he'd spent more than an hour, looking at Kashish's videos, and her perfect, flawless face, at the way she lifted an eyebrow, at her shiny hair, and then he'd spent another hour looking at the skit videos she posted and smiling at some of them, despite himself.

The way her personality transformed was amazing. In those videos, she was Aunty K, a married woman in her thirties who had a nauseatingly perfect husband (played by her) and two kids (also played by her). The kids were total brats, but to Aunty K, they were angels, the epitome of good behaviour. Aunty K was respectful to everyone in her family and she was the model of the perfect Indian Muslim bahu.

But somehow, in each video, it felt like Kashish was sharing an inside joke with the audience, and he got the appeal. It made him want to be her friend, the way she implied her audience were her friends. Aunty K was a silly and simpering woman and he wanted her to know that he got what she was trying to say in the videos, even though he couldn't quite articulate it. He was also gobsmacked by the number of views her videos got. The one she'd made of him already had 2 million views!

He got sucked into reading the stream of comments below the video. Some laughed, quite a few defended him. Most of these people had started following him.

He really should have left it at that.

But no, he had to go and begin a war with Kashish Asif, Internet celebrity (what if he'd never heard of her until this morning). A war in which he was at fault.

'Some really bad editing software,' Sameer replied miserably.

'Listen, you post an apology and it should be fine,' Sadeem said earnestly.

Sameer looked at him, desperately needing to believe that everything would be fine.

'You think?'

Sadeem's hesitation cemented what he'd already guessed. 'People can't download the video, can they?' he asked, uncertainly. He was clearly not as skilled at Instagram as his younger brother.

'They can, and they have,' Sadeem said quietly.

Shit.

'People are adding their own two bits to the end of that video and posting it on their accounts. They're sharing it on WhatsApp.'

'What the…'

'Your follower count got bumped up by a good number but you're also getting a lot of hate comments,' Sadeem remarked.

Sameer's stomach twisted.

'I want to delete my account. I don't want to be on Instagram any longer.'

Sadeem stared at him.

'You don't mean that.'

'I do,' Sameer said.

Sadeem shook his head. 'Look, these things happen. People make mistakes. And you're just nineteen. You didn't know any better. Post an apology and move on. Deleting the reel was a good idea, but deleting your account gives the wrong message.'

'You're just seventeen. How do you know all this?' Sameer asked, trying not to think of how he'd destroyed everything in the span of a thirty-second video.

'Because I just do. It's not the end of the world. Without the caption, it actually did seem funny.'

'Only if you have the mental capacity of a five year old,' Sameer groaned.

'That's okay. You're allowed to make mistakes as long as you accept that you made a mistake.'

The two of them sat in silence for a moment, and then Sadeem got up. 'I'll think of something to post, something to counter the video. And I promise, things will be fine.'

Sameer sighed. 'Thank god Ammi and Abbu aren't on Instagram.'

Sadeem shuddered. 'Imagine if our parents saw that video.'

Sameer mirrored his shudder. 'They'd take away our phones for good.' He turned to his brother who was headed to their room to take a shower. 'You really think I should stay on Instagram?'

Sadeem paused and turned around. 'Look, I'm not going to tell you that it's going to be easy to accept your mistake and make an apology video. But you need to do it. People can't think that you condone domestic violence. You went too far with the atta analogy. But social media, especially Instagram, will help your YouTube channel and you want that, right? This repository thing you were going on about? So you're going to have to keep at it. This is a blip.'

Two hours later, they had recorded and uploaded a video in which Sameer apologised to Kashish. By the time it was done, he was exhausted. How did Kashish have the energy to make and post so many videos? She was so versatile, and funny, and despite the fact that she'd started the war by mocking him, he had become a reluctant fan.

They heard the gate creak open. Ammi must have come home. Abbu would be coming in a little later. They were going to Vellore tomorrow to talk to Ammajan, and convince her to come stay with them for a few days.

'Let's hope this works and this is the end of this spat,' Sadeem said, as he rubbed the back of his neck. 'I'm famished.'

'What do you want to eat?' Sameer asked with a sigh, thinking of rustling something up for all of them for dinner.

Sadeem didn't respond. He was staring at his phone, a dismayed expression on his face. The gate outside creaked shut and Sameer could hear the locks on the main door disengaging as Ammi unlocked it.

'What happened?' Sameer asked.

'She's posted a rebuttal,' Sadeem said softly.

'Already?' Sameer asked incredulously. They'd posted their apology video just moments ago.

'Fifteen minutes ago. We were too busy editing and uploading ours,' Sadeem said curtly.

'How bad is it?'

Sadeem looked up at him.

'Bad.'

10

There were three people in Kashish's room, apart from her. Rania and Jessie were checking their phones nervously, while Mili was watching them all from the screen on Kashish's laptop.

'It's fine. It's fine,' she kept saying. 'I just wish you'd told me before.'

Kashish was lying on her bed, staring at the ceiling. She was exhausted. 'I know Mili. I'm sorry I cracked open your schedule. But I just…' She trailed off.

The video she'd posted a while ago was gaining traction. She had abandoned all gimmicks and funny moments, and instead opted to make a serious video about domestic violence offering statistics, interspersing it with clips of her face in the atta ball getting whacked on Sameer's counter.

Rania tugged her ankle.

'He posted an apology.'

Kashish sat up. 'Good for him.'

Rania looked up from the phone. 'I think he's realised his mistake and you needn't have schooled him.'

Kashish shrugged. 'It's done. I'm not deleting my video.'

She glanced at Jessie who was packing up the equipment and calling it a day. Jessie helped her out with the shoots and was her assistant of sorts. She even handled enquiries about collaborations and spoke to sponsors on behalf of Kashish.

Jessie looked up. 'I saw the video too. He sounds genuinely apologetic. You should go easy on him.'

'Why?' Kashish asked, annoyed. 'Because he's good looking?'

Jessie's face flushed. Everyone knew that she fell in love with a new person, literally every week. She wore her heart on her sleeve and she was not afraid of loving openly, over and over again. In fact, that was how she and Kashish had met. She'd come to Kashish and told her that she was in love with her. Kashish had let her down gently, saying she wasn't interested, only to find her confessing her love to someone else in a few days. And it went on.

'No, because he seems sincere,' Jessie said. 'Anyway, I'm off. Please don't do another rebuttal video. I don't think my brain can handle it.'

Kashish didn't reply. She'd already had an earful from Mili for disrupting her schedule. She was supposed to post a reel about a new bookstore-cafe and instead, she'd gone on this silly war with an unknown Instagrammer.

'It's late. I have to go too,' Rania said, checking her phone. She blew out a breath. 'It's over. Stop it now. Okay?'

Kashish nodded but then she narrowed her eyes. 'I will if he does.'

Rania rolled her eyes. 'Hey, just sort it out on DM.'

Kashish's eyes widened. 'No way. Let *him* reach out to me if he wants to end this.'

Rania was almost at the door when she turned around. 'What started this? Like why did you even begin?'

Kashish couldn't remember now. She shrugged.

'Did he do anything to instigate you?' Rania insisted.

Kashish shook her head. 'Please. If it's anyone's fault, it must be Instagram's algorithm's fault.'

Then she thought of the video she had seen earlier with Kinza, where she'd seen Sameer cook chicken Chettinad. 'Actually, my sister was watching a video of him on YouTube,' she remarked.

'And that pissed you off?'

Kashish shook her head again. 'No. I don't know. Something. I woke up in the middle of the night.' Crying.

She'd woken up crying, missing her mother with an almost physical ache, missing her sister who was sleeping in the adjacent room with another ache that she couldn't quite explain.

Poor Sameer had just been in the wrong place at the wrong time. But what he'd done was also not right and she'd seen the video shared in multiple places, accompanied with that cackling male laughter that always put her nerves on edge.

When the house was empty, and she knew it was going to be at least another hour before Abbu came home, she did something she rarely did.

She called Kinza.

'Api?'

'Hey, how are you?' Kinza asked. Her voice was drowned by the sound of the mixie whirring and then shutting down immediately. 'Sorry, sorry. I'm stepping out of the kitchen.'

Before Kashish could say anything, Kinza yelled. 'I said no eating snacks before dinner. WHO gave you that Munch?'

Kashish shut her eyes briefly, out of exasperation, but also because she could imagine the expression on her sister's face.

'Okay, ya, I'm back. Tell me,' Kinza said.

'I…' Kashish didn't know why she had called her. Kinza had left just a couple of days ago. Normally, they spoke on the phone once or twice a month, and that too, only if she answered Abbu's phone when he was in the loo, or something. Kinza didn't call her and neither did she call her sister. So this was new to them.

'All good?'

Kashish sighed. The day-to-day minutiae of her life that she wanted to convey to her sister felt futile and silly now. Especially as she knew her sister was going to get called away at any moment.

'Yeah, all good.'

'Munni, I was serious about you coming and staying here for a few days,' Kinza said.

'I don't know,' Kashish said, still not used to Kinza using her childhood nickname.

'Munni stinks! Munni stinks!'

'Shush! Stop that, Kabir! I'm sorry about that!' Kinza apologised quickly. 'Why are you so doubtful about coming here?'

'But why do you want me to come there?' Kashish persisted.

'I want to spend time with you. Get to know you. The little I see of you every year at vacations isn't enough!'

Kashish's eyebrows went up. 'Let me see,' she was sure she would regret going there, and she would come back from Chennai missing Kinza even more.

'Oh yay! Now tell me why you really called. Is it because of a boy?' Kinza asked, her voice lowered conspiratorially.

'Well, sort of. But not in the way you think!' Kashish said quickly before Kinza started adding up all the possibilities.

'Then what way is there?' Kinza sounded baffled.

'Api, please. It's a professional situation,' Kashish said, aware of how grown up and important she sounded. She really hoped Kinza wouldn't make fun of her or laugh at her.

'Oh. Okay. I'm sorry. Tell me. How can I help?'

'If someone makes fun of you, and then you make fun of them, and then they make fun of you again, when does it stop?'

Kinza listened in silence and then burst out laughing. 'Who started it?' she asked.

Kashish winced. 'I did.'

'What?'

'Yeah, I started it and it became something and now it's snowballed into something else.'

'Then just stop it, Munni,' Kinza said, as if it were that easy. Her friends had said that too. But if he posted something about her again, she wasn't going to be responsible for her actions, she decided.

'Okay. I'll stop it. But if he does it again…'

'Just call and talk to him and end it,' Kinza said, as if it was the most reasonable thing in the world.

'Call and talk to him?' Kashish choked out the words.

'Yeah? Why?'

'I can't *call* him!' Kashish replied. 'It's absurd. I don't *call* anyone.' Not even you. She couldn't imagine picking up the phone and actually calling Sameer. The very idea gave her goosebumps for some reason.

'Things are so much easier these days. Just send him a message then,' Kinza suggested.

This was also what Rania had said to her. 'No, I'm not sending him a message,' Kashish said firmly.

'Ah, it's an ego thing,' Kinza said. 'Who's this guy? I want to check him out.'

'No one important,' Kashish said quickly. She was afraid that her sister would get on Instagram to see Sameer and somehow end up seeing all her videos.

When she'd first started making those skits, she was half-afraid that Kinza would discover that she was the inspiration for Aunty K and would be mad at her. But Kinza never had time for social media. She was too busy running the house, looking after the kids, cooking and what not. Whatever free time she had, she didn't spend it on social media.

Kashish almost envied that existence. Almost.

'When do your holidays begin?' Kinza asked, thankfully moving on from the subject of the fight.

'Why?'

'So I can book your ticket.'

She really was serious, then, Kashish thought, feeling something warm in her belly.

'Come on, Munni. It will be fun. Do some of your videos and reels here in Chennai. It will be a change for your fans too.'

That clinched it.

'Okay, I'll come and stay for a few days,' she said.

'Good. I've already spoken with Abbu and he's happy we're spending time together.'

'But he'll be alone here,' Kashish protested.

'It's okay. He'll be fine,' Kinza said breezily.

Kashish didn't know why she felt loads better after talking to her sister who hadn't given her anything new to work with about the situation with Sameer. If anything, she'd repeated what Rania told her.

She ended the call. Using the phone for a call had been odd. Her fingers automatically tapped open Instagram.

There were a few thousand DMs sitting in her messages inbox and she knew Jessie would take care of them, weeding out all the crap from the important messages. Her finger hovered over it in any case and then she tapped it open.

She wasn't going to DM Sameer Ehsan. He could go suck an egg. He could fly a kite. He could slip and fall into a puddle. He could…

He had DM'd her.

11

The journey from Chennai to Vellore was roughly two hours long, and Sameer had spent a majority of those two hours listening to his brother go on and on about how he was making his job as his social media manager redundant.

'You could have at least told me that you were planning to DM her,' he said for the hundred and fiftieth time.

'And you would have stopped me,' Sameer remarked, looking out of the window. He barely registered the winding highway in the distance.

'Because how well did your plan work out?' Sadeem asked. He crumpled the packet of chips and pushed it inside his backpack.

'She didn't block me,' Sameer said with a shrug. He'd been surprised that she hadn't, which made him think that she wanted to keep the lines of communication between them open.

'She didn't reply to you either. Left you on seen,' Sadeem reminded him.

'That's okay.'

'It's not. But fine, I get it. You wanted to end this. So let's move on. And even if she does do something, please, please for the love of God, just let her do it.'

Sameer shifted in his hard seat. 'That's not fair.'

'Life is not fair. She's been in this far longer than you have. She's got sponsors and partnerships and whatnot. You are just a minnow. She's a shark. Let her get away with whatever she wants while you do your thing.'

'Which is?' Sameer sighed.

'Make those videos. Convince Ammajan to come back with us. We can record some snippets of her saying those mean things she says to you and use them at the end of all the videos. It can be like our signature,' Sadeem said, sounding excited.

'Fine. Okay. Let's do this,' Sameer put his head back on the head rest and shut his eyes. His mind took him to that reckless moment when he'd sent Kashish the DM.

He had watched her video chastising him, over and over again, and it made him feel like a fool. He should not have let his anger lead him and he wanted to apologise to her in person. But she lived in Bangalore and anyway, why would she even agree to meet him? He was the idiot who had put her face on a blob of atta.

He hadn't stopped to think. He had just typed out a message:

> I'm sorry for the video. I didn't know what I was thinking. I didn't realise how it sounded until much later and I pulled it down. Again, apologies.

Then he hit send and waited. His stomach cramped painfully as he thought of what she would say. Would she reply? Would she block him? He was willing to take it because he deserved it.

His fingers tingled when he could see that she was online but he held back from writing to her again, just so she could see his message. She'd already seen his earlier one and hadn't replied.

That was the only good thing he'd done, according to Sadeem.

'She would have certainly blocked you if you wrote to her repeatedly,' he said.

Well, best to think how they would convince Ammajan and bring her to Chennai with them. They'd already told her their plans on the phone and she had laughed them off. As Ammi suggested, he had dangled the lure of Fiza's cousin's wedding which got her attention.

'Kitte din hogey shaadi ku jaako,' Ammajan said, sounding wistful. Sameer couldn't help but grin. The pandemic hadn't stopped weddings from taking place, but it had drastically reduced the number of guests. For people like his grandmother, weddings were the place they could socialise and meet their friends and relatives. It must have been so tedious for her, especially during the lockdowns.

He glanced at his brother and saw that he was asleep. They would be reaching Vellore soon enough. He pulled out his phone from his jeans pocket and opened Instagram, his heart thudding so loudly, it sounded in his ears. There were around a hundred DMs.

Shit.

He was not used to handling all this. His disastrous video had led to the wrong sort of people following him, and he wasn't sure how to disengage from them all.

He tapped open the inbox. There were countless message requests. Some of these were people lauding him for accepting his mistake and being real about it. Others were pissed that he had apologised and that there was nothing wrong with the video. And there were some who were still hating him for taking on their darling Kashish.

Ouch.

He rubbed the side of his neck anxiously as he went to the message that he'd sent Kashish. She wasn't going to reply to him. But still, he tapped it open, and to his shock, she was online and he could see that she was typing something.

His scalp prickled. He considered waking up Sadeem for a moment. But then his gaze was back to the message. Would she rip him a new one for the video? He had to remind himself that she was the one who had started it all by mocking him. He'd done nothing till then but exist in a quiet corner of his world and the internet, until she had decided to make fun of him.

But he didn't type. He wanted to first see what she would say. His heartbeat sounded unnaturally loud in his ears. His mouth was dry. He had to stay composed and not make a fool of himself.

His mind offered suggestions on how to respond, but unless he could see what she wrote, how could he come up with a counter response?

Had she looked at his videos, he wondered. Had she seen the earlier stuff he'd posted? What had she made of him? Did she think he was an idiot overall?

The message popped up in his inbox.

Ok

12

Kashish stared at the group texts on her phone as the car sped along the highway. Abbu was driving, a half-smile on his face, as if he was contemplating something privately. Instead of syncing their phones to the car's Bluetooth and in turn, connecting to her Spotify playlist, Abbu had fitted an old USB drive he'd rustled from somewhere and the songs were playing out sequentially.

Kashish winced and looked out of the window.

'Tu mera, tu mera, hero no. 1!'

Her father, staid and respectful and even boring, was a closet Govinda fan, and he *loved* trashy Hindi music from the '90s. So had her mother, and Kashish remembered Ammi singing along loudly on these road trips. She had been eight or nine then, and thought it was very funny. If she'd been any older, she would have fainted of embarrassment as her mother belted out 'Main majnu majnu chillaungi, kurta phaad ke'.

Right now though, Kashish was dissolving in second-hand embarrassment for her father. But she was also going to put this on her reels. So she'd taken shots of him singing along, jiggling his shoulders, and even as she had laughed more than she had in a long time, she felt a twang in the middle of her chest.

'You'll be okay?' she asked him.

He glanced at her.

'Of course, I will. Why won't I be?'

She sighed. 'But you'll be all alone in the house.'

'It's fine, Kashish. You enjoy your holiday with your sister. I'm so glad you're going. I'm so glad you two are connecting again.'

Kashish didn't respond to that. She looked down at her lap and flipped her phone over and over. Then she opened the group chat and read the messages. Most were from Jessie informing her that she would try and schedule some collaborations with any cafes and the like in Chennai. Some were from Mili, reminding her to not mess with her list again. Rania, however, had one word of advice.

Have fun. This stuff will keep happening.

Yeah right.

She had to stay on top of her game. She couldn't slip up now. But there were times when she wasn't sure where she was going with this. The million followers benchmark had changed things for her. For how long, and to what end, were questions she didn't have answers to.

Kinza had been thrilled when she heard that Abbu was dropping off Kashish and he'd reluctantly agreed to stay for a day before returning to Bangalore. On the phone, Kinza had said that it would be just like the old times. But how, Kashish wondered. How could anything be like the old times?

Still, she'd been a good sport, packing her stuff, making sure to carry some formal dresses as well, because Kinza told her there would be a wedding that she would have to attend. The very idea of attending a wedding made Kashish's hackles rise.

A week ago, she and Rania sat in her room, where she showed the message Sameer had sent her. Rania tried her best to decipher it and finally came up with nothing.

'I think he's one of those guys who's actually saying what he means,' she said.

'You think?'

Rania nodded. 'He's apologetic about it. And I think you should let it go.'

'I did,' Kashish said. 'See? I said "ok" to him. I let it go.'

Rania didn't say anything at first.

'What?'

'Nothing.'

'No, tell me what?'

'Don't you think you made this into a big issue? Not the atta video,' she clarified quickly.

'Then?'

'You singled him out when he had done nothing to you.'

Kashish rolled her eyes. 'Yeah, I told you, I was feeling shitty that day. I didn't know what got into me. I did it. Regretted it for like five seconds, and then moved on.'

'I was thinking…' Rania said, as she swiped up the screen.

'That's never a good thing,' Kashish joked.

'Shut up. I was thinking that since you're going to be in Chennai, you should reach out to him. Do a collab video with him.'

Kashish stared at her like she was crazy, which she had to be if she was suggesting something like that.

'Come on, it's not a bad idea,' Rania went on.

Kashish shook her head. 'First of all, why would I reach out to him? And why on earth should I dilute my brand by connecting it with his?'

Rania rolled her eyes. 'Look at you. Talking about "your brand" and all. I just thought it would be a fun thing to do. Both your followers will enjoy it I'm sure.'

Kashish shook her head. 'Um, not after I called him out for promoting domestic violence.'

Rania's face fell but then she brightened up. 'It can be a way of letting bygones be bygones.'

'No. I'm not going to reach out to him. I don't know him at all. The very idea makes me uncomfortable,' she said.

Rania pursed her lips and nodded. 'Okay, but what if you *do* get to know him? See? He's posted so many videos after that, and each one ends with his Nani either twisting his ear, or pinching his cheek, all affectionately mind you, and it's so cute.'

Kashish knew what she meant. She'd reluctantly watched the videos too, after sending him that 'ok', which felt like she'd thrown a line into the water and was waiting for a fish to bite. But he hadn't texted her after that and she told herself she wasn't secretly disappointed. This was exactly where she wanted to leave things.

So, Rania's suggestion of looking him up, sending him a DM and asking to meet him in a coffee shop and then proposing they do a collaboration was not something she was going to do. She was horrified by the prospect of it.

Rania sighed. 'Fine. Don't reach out to him. I wish *I* was going to Chennai. He's so cute.'

'I'm sure Aamir would have something to say to that,' Kashish reminded her archly and Rania didn't stop or put her hand to cover Kashish's mouth because they weren't in her house. They could talk freely about Rania's boyfriend, Aamir, here. But Rania blushed and rolled her eyes.

'I meant he's cute for *you*.'

'No. Way.' Kashish protested. Rania looked at her shrewdly.

'Okay. Fine. But here's a piece of advice, Kashish,' Rania said.

'Yes, oh wise one. Please enlighten me,' Kashish said, pressing her palms together and lowering her head.

'Stop being such an ass.'

Kashish's heart had jumped in her chest at Rania's suggestion but she brought it under control remarkably quickly.

'Anything else?' she asked, lifting her head slightly.

'And be open to new experiences!'

'For the vlog?'

Rania did a face-palm. 'No. For life. Okay?'

Now here she was, looking out of the window as the highway sped past them. On the music system, Govinda was singing, 'Akhiyon se goli maare', and Abbu was singing along.

She was going to take Rania's advice and see where life led her.

13

'I wouldn't say it's perfect, but it comes pretty close.'

Sameer rolled his eyes at his brother as he drained the last of the dal vadais on a paper napkin. 'You are *too* much, do you know that?'

'Of course. But given where I've taken your Instagram account, you should be grateful that I'm working for peanuts.' Sadeem fiddled with the phone camera taking some close-up shots of the dish.

Ammajan was sitting at the kitchen island, watching a loud Pakistani show on her phone, shelling peas as she did it. She looked up at both of them.

'I'm trying to hear the dialogues!' she said, irritably.

'Here. You should use this,' Sadeem said, offering her wireless ear buds. She swatted them away.

'That will fall out of my ears and I'll step on one and that's it. I don't like these things hanging out of my ears.'

Sadeem and Sameer shared a look. While it was wonderful having Ammajan stay with them, Sadeem sometimes groaned that Ammajan was the human equivalent of a cat in more ways than one. She hardly moved out from the kitchen island, preferring to sit there and watch shows on her phone while she did small chores. This meant Sadeem couldn't shoot Sameer's videos as easily.

The few times they managed to shoot the videos, she had butted in asking questions, offering suggestions, making faces whenever the camera shifted to her. It was a wonder they had managed to accomplish anything at all.

'Ammajan, we need you to record another snippet with Bhai,' Sadeem said. Ammajan made a face.

'How much you boys make me work. For FREE,' she grumbled.

'But think of the wedding you're going to go to this evening. It will be worth all this hassle,' Sameer reminded her.

'That wedding is the only reason I came,' she announced loftily and turned to Sadeem immediately. 'Don't you dare put your hand on your heart and pretend like I hurt you.'

'You're too sharp for us, Ammajan,' Sadeem protested.

'Chalo, what do you want me to do?' she asked.

'We already recorded the video and…'

'I saw,' she said, wryly. 'If he has to cook, he should look like a bawarchi, no? What is this rolling of sleeves he does each time?'

Sameer blushed, and then glared at Sadeem whose idea it had been. Since he wasn't wearing tight T shirts any longer, (not because Kashish had made fun of him, but because it wasn't his comfort zone), Sadeem had hit upon this idea to make him look sexy but in an understated way.

So, for each video, they spent precious seconds while he rolled up his sleeves. As much as Sameer hated to admit it to his brother, it did seem to work, because the views for his videos had jumped drastically. He had finally found his niche. He was the good boy-nerd-who-liked-to-cook but he was also book-boyfriend-material, at least according to his younger brother who seemed to have a better idea of all this than him.

'Ammajan, girls love it when he rolls his sleeves. It's apparently a thing.'

'A thing?' she asked, eyebrows drawn together.

'Yeah, to make him look sexy without trying too hard.'

'Tauba, look at you, saying all this in front of me!' Ammajan said, blushing. 'Chalo, what do you need me to do? I can pinch his bum if you want.'

Poor Sameer who had been clearing the counter, accidentally knocked over a jug of water.

'Ammajan! He's your *grandson*!' Sadeem said, shocked.

'Yes, and I've washed his bum many times when he was small. So I can pinch it too,' she retorted.

Sameer glared at his brother as if it was all his fault. He pulled out a few kitchen towels from the dispenser and wiped the counter clean.

'No one is pinching my bum,' he said, just as Ammi walked inside. Her face lit up when she saw all of them in the kitchen.

'Something smells good. And what is this talk of pinching bums?' she asked.

'Nothing,' Sameer said quickly. 'I just made a batch of dal vadais for a video. And for an evening snack. Want some?'

Ammi nodded eagerly, and sat down next to Ammajan. 'Ammi, it's so nice to have you here,' she said, putting her head on Ammajan's shoulder. Sameer felt an odd pinch in his chest, a reminder that his mother was a daughter too. Ammajan, of course, was not fooled by any sentimentality.

'You're only saying that because I'm making all your favourite dishes with these boys here,' she said gruffly.

Ammi rolled her eyes. 'I wish we didn't have to go to that wedding,' she sighed. 'I'm so tired. But it's Nadia Bhabhi's niece's wedding and she'll never talk to me if I don't go.'

'The wedding is tomorrow. It's the haldi today,' Ammajan reminded her with delight. Ammi groaned.

'Noooo...I have to dress up tomorrow also?'

'Yes, you do,' Ammajan retorted as she pushed her chair back and stood up. 'I'm going to get ready now.'

'We have to leave for the haldi at 8 p.m. It's only six now!' Ammi protested.

'It takes that long for me to get ready,' Ammajan said. Sameer and Sadeem were busy checking the video they'd just shot when Ammajan turned to him.

'You two better be dressed and on your best behaviour, okay?' she said. 'No more of this sexy business and all.' She blushed even as she said it.

'But why do *we* have to come?' Sadeem groaned out aloud.

'You have to. That's it. Maybe you can shoot some videos there,' Ammajan said. When she left the kitchen, Ammi and the boys shared a look with each other. Then, with a sigh, Ammi pulled the plate of dal vadais close and picked up one and bit into it.

'At least no one has to make dinner tonight,' she said.

Neither of the boys responded.

14

'You're sure it's fine if I attend this wedding, considering I wasn't even invited?' Kashish asked Kinza, as she sat at the dressing table in the guest room where she had been staying for the past week or so since she arrived in Chennai.

'I've told you like fifty times. This is a close family wedding, and as my sister, you are invited by default because I will be there, right?' Kinza said, bending down to look at her reflection in the mirror.

'You look so different,' Kashish murmured. Kinza was dressed in a light pink shalwar kurta that dazzled with stone work and some light diamond jewellery to accentuate it.

'Good different or bad different?' Kinza asked.

'Good different only,' Kashish said with a rare smile. Kinza's face lit up.

'We should take a selfie,' Kinza said, blinking.

'We should. But let me get ready first.' Kashish went back to touching up her face with a brush.

'That looks like you're not doing anything and it doesn't look like you have any makeup on, but I just saw you slather on so much of whatever you squeezed out of that tube,' Kinza commented.

Aunty K discovers makeup.

Aunty K learns the difference between millennials and Gen Z.

Aunty K frets over not feeding fresh dosas to her family.

The ideas had been pouring in ever since Kashish came here. She had jotted them all down in her notebook and hoped to remember the details when she eventually shot the videos back in Bangalore.

She had been a reluctant guest initially, especially awkward around Kaif Bhai while the kids warmed up to her quickly enough. But Kashish cherished the moments when the family was out of the house and it was just the two of them.

She and Kinza spent lazy mornings watching TV while Kinza dished out hot parathas, or homemade fluffy idlis and with each bite, the resentment that had built in her heart over the years crumbled a little more. But there was also dread for the day she would have to return to Bangalore and face real life without her sister. She'd do it but it would still destroy her a little, to go back to that existence.

While the majority of the day was their own, where Kashish hung out in the kitchen watching her sister cook, unconsciously noting her mannerisms for the Aunty K videos, once it was mid-afternoon, she could sense her sister slip away from her, ever so slowly.

First, it was the kids coming back from school. Kabir was home first but he was no bother, Kashish discovered.

Kinza would bathe him, feed him and he'd go down like a light for his afternoon nap. Kinza turned into mom mode fully when Kainaat returned from school.

There was the same bathing and feeding followed by homework and projects and reluctantly, Kashish found herself sitting down with her niece, helping her with her craft projects.

Kaif Bhai came back from work at around six in the evenings, and seeing Kinza in wife mode made her most uncomfortable. She did not enjoy seeing her sister run around, first to freshen up and get ready before her husband returned. She kept his tea ready, and after he showered, the two of them would spend an hour talking quietly in the living room while Kashish felt like an interloper.

She liked Kaif Bhai. She just didn't like the person her sister became when he was at home. She was constantly anticipating his needs, always looking for ways to make him happy and while she knew he made her sister happy in many ways, Kashish didn't understand why she tried so hard.

She had even asked Kinza about it once, over breakfast.

'He sees you like this, in the housecoat in the mornings. So why all that effort to look nice in the evenings?' she asked, chewing her dosa. 'And he's seen you through two childbirths. He's seen you at your worst. *And* he was your boyfriend before you got married.'

'So?' Kinza asked.

'So shouldn't you be comfortable and be the way you are all the time? Why all this effort?'

Kinza shrugged. 'Because I like it.'

'Wait, so you don't do it because he likes it and expects you to be a particular way?' Kashish asked, frowning.

'He does, but *I* also like to dress up. For him,' Kinza had said with a big smile. Kashish groaned internally.

'Is everyone ready?' Kaif Bhai called.

Kashish stood up and smoothed the fabric of her anarkali gown. 'You're sure this isn't too much?'

Kinza shook her head. 'Once you see the others there, you'll know you're underdressed. Are you sure you don't want to wear some of my jewellery?'

'No way. Let's go,' Kashish said, just as Kabir came barrelling into the room and knocked into her knee. What do you know. The little brat looked adorable today. He was dressed in a light blue shirt with sleeves rolled up, brown corduroys, and a suspender. And his hair had been slicked back with gel.

'Oh my god, who is this handsome young man?' Kashish asked, her hand on her chest in an exaggerated manner. Thankfully, he did not ruin the effect by doing something awful. Instead, he gave her a shy smile and lifted up his arms, indicating that he wanted to be carried.

'No Kabir! You're getting too big to be carried!' Kinza said, shaking her head.

'One minute won't do any harm,' Kashish said as she bent to pick him up. He threw his arms around her neck and kissed her cheek. Like the rapidly melting glaciers in the Arctic, Kashish found her defences breaking down too.

'Time for a selfie,' she said, clearing her throat.

15

'Isn't this usually reserved for close family members?' Sameer whispered in Sadeem's ear as they made their way towards the glittering house in the distance.

'Well, Ammajan is close for them, right?' his brother replied with a shrug.

'And we also get to tag along,' Sameer said with a sigh. He was not looking forward to this at all. Weddings were boring events and the only thing that made them worth attending was the biryani. But this was the haldi that usually went on late into the night, well after the biryani was eaten and digested.

Ammajan was sprightly, dressed in a cream silk saree, the saree pallu covering her head demurely, as if she had not just suggested pinching her grandson's bottom earlier that evening. Sameer had parked the car in one of the lanes.

The four of them made their way to the house slowly. Abbu would be joining them later as he hadn't yet returned from work. Ammi had been muttering she wouldn't have minded a late evening meeting today, and Ammajan had glared at her but hadn't said anything.

'If it gets too boring, can I just escape to the beach?' Sameer asked.

Ammi turned around to give him a look.

'No. If I can't escape, neither can you,' she said succinctly.

'It's not fair when we're so close to the beach and…' he paused. Another family was near the gate as well, and he didn't want to sound like a sulking six year old.

Fairy lights twinkled all along the sides of the house, like a pulsing collection of stars. Sameer geared himself for a night of socialising that usually involved people asking what he was studying and why he wasn't doing engineering. Then they would turn to Sadeem, and tell him patronisingly that they hoped at least he would study engineering.

The other family had gone inside the gate but they hadn't reached the house yet.

'Kinza?' Ammi called out. The lady turned around and Sameer noted she was really pretty. She looked vaguely familiar in the way most of these women did, and he suppressed a sigh, as he glanced at the two kids, each holding on to their father's hand. Another girl was with them but she stood at a distance.

'Misba Apa! So nice to see you!' the lady, Kinza, said. She turned towards her family, but they had already moved closer to the house.

Ammi and Kinza started talking, and Ammajan made a noise of impatience.

'Oh Aunty! Sorry, sorry! Let's go inside and talk,' Kinza suggested, holding on to Ammajan's elbow. Somewhat mollified, Ammajan made her way up the steps with Kinza by her side, Ammi on her other side, still talking.

Sadeem and Sameer climbed the steps slowly when Kinza paused at the door. 'Oh, I forgot to introduce you all to my little sister. Kashish!' she called out. The other girl who was lingering just inside the door turned.

'Let's go inside first,' Ammajan said, bemused at all this chatter happening on the steps of the house.

But Sameer froze. Kashish? It had to be a coincidence that the name that haunted him every day for the past couple of weeks was…right here.

Sadeem slammed into him from the back because he'd stopped short on the steps. He turned around to look at his brother, his eyes wide and worried.

Shit. Shit. Shit.

He had never thought he would meet her face to face. At least not like this.

'What is it?' Sadeem asked. Grabbing his wrist, Sameer pulled him away from there.

'Where are you guys going?' Ammi called out, annoyance evident in her voice.

Sameer didn't reply. He led a reluctant Sadeem from there.

'It's Kashish,' he said when they were back near the gate.

Sadeem blinked. 'Who?'

'That lady, Kinza's sister. It's Kashish Asif. My Instagram nemesis,' he explained.

Sadeem's mouth dropped open and then it became an 'O'. Then he narrowed his eyes. 'So you ran from there?' he asked.

'I…I didn't…'

He had. He had run from there, like a coward.

'Okay. I just needed a moment to process it,' he breathed out. 'We can go back now.'

'Did she see you?' Sadeem asked.

'I don't know,' Sameer admitted, his heart thumping loudly. He hadn't even seen her clearly but he just knew it was her.

'I'm such an idiot.'

'Hard to disagree,' Sadeem said cheerfully.

'Let's go back.'

'Why are you like this?'

'Like what?'

'You're not being yourself right now. You're acting like a…oh my god, you have a crush on an internet celebrity,' Sadeem chortled.

'That's rubbish,' Sameer said severely. 'Let's go.'

Feeling somewhat composed—*crush? no way, ridiculous, and she was his nemesis, and yes, there were times she appeared in his head without any reason*—he and Sadeem made their way back inside the house. His mother and grandmother had been swallowed by the hordes of people around them, and suddenly the prospect of this evening wasn't boring.

It was terrifying.

It was exhilarating.

'Look at you,' Sadeem murmured.

'Why? Do I have something on my face?' Sameer asked quickly.

'No, you idiot. You need to dial back the anxiety a little. It's fine. She's just a girl.'

Just a girl, he mentally scoffed at his brother.

Just a girl who happens to have a million followers, has been mentioned in several listicles (that he happened to come across while googling her for no reason whatsoever), has been interviewed by an RJ on a live radio show, and someone who happens to appear in his dreams, every now and then. Dreams that he cannot recall without blushing.

No, no, no. This is normal teenage stuff, right? So what if he was nearly twenty? This didn't have to mean anything.

Inside the house, he looked around casually, trying to slow his racing heartbeat. He was really being an ass about all of this. He should be a little more pissed at her. Hadn't she cherry picked him and mocked him for no reason whatsoever? *But that had led to a substantial bump in his followers.* But then hadn't she made him look like an lowlife incel who promoted domestic violence? *Well, he'd deserved it.*

He breathed in and out. The haldi function was nowhere near beginning right now. Men and women were often segregated, and there wouldn't be much chance for him to see any of the women. If he was so lucky…or unlucky.

He was certainly unlucky if he didn't get to speak to her and apologise in person, his mind informed him.

What an excellent excuse to talk to the girl who had ridiculed him in front of her one million followers. Right?

Sadeem nudged his elbow.

'Stop trying to be like Superman.'

'What?' he asked, startled.

'You're trying to x-ray vision your way into the ladies' section,' Sadeem informed him.

‘I am not,’ Sameer huffed out. But he followed his brother into the open hall of the bungalow, which was lined with chairs along the sides and they found a place to sit.

He really was a fool. Instead of introducing himself, he had run away, and now he didn’t know if he would see her again. Would she be coming tomorrow? The way his heart jumped was hard to ignore.

His brother leaned close. ‘Send her a DM. Tell her you saw her here.’

Sameer sat back in the chair and shook his head. ‘Sometimes, you have the worst ideas, Sadeem, but then your brain isn’t fully developed, so it’s excusable.’

Sadeem looked affronted. ‘What? Why?’

‘She’s at this function with her sister. I don’t think she’d appreciate a stalker-y DM from me.’

‘But how is it stalker-y?’ Sadeem asked.

Sameer cocked his head. ‘Come on. Think of it from her point of view,’ he said quietly.

Sadeem sighed and his shoulders fell. ‘Shit. Yeah. I didn’t realise. You’re right.’

‘Hell must have frozen over because you admitted I’m right,’ Sameer said with a grin. But his gaze was still fixed to the wooden partition behind which all the ladies were disappearing.

16

In the car, Kashish had been quiet, as she took in the city. They had been out a few times late at night for ice creams, and once to Marina Beach but it was so crowded and she didn't even get a glimpse of the sea, so it hadn't felt like much.

Kinza chattered on happily. They were going to Besantnagar, one of the posh areas of Chennai, and the beach was nearby. She turned to Kaif and said laughingly, 'Perhaps one day we will have a home here!' Kaif Bhai only chuckled nervously in reply.

Kashish smiled to herself. She hoped Kaif Bhai would make enough money one day to be able to afford it. As someone who lived in a land-bound city, it astonished her that people who lived near the water spent their entire lives being able to stare out at the beach whenever they felt like it. And they hardly ever even went to the beach!

'Can we go to the beach later?' she asked. At this, Kainaat and Kabir both started chanting 'Beach! Beach!' Kinza shuddered.

'We'll come to the beach another day, Munni. Not now. There's no time and it will be dark. Anyway we can't go to the beach in these clothes.'

'I want beach!' Kabir said adamantly and Kashish winced, feeling like an idiot for bringing up the beach *now*. What had she been thinking.

'Later. Not now,' Kaif admonished him and Kabir fell silent. They reached the grandiose house and as they stepped out of the car, Kashish gasped. A blast of humid air hit her like a wet sack.

'Do you people wear different makeup here? Humidity-proof?' she asked Kinza as they walked towards the house. There were sparkling lights everywhere, and the house was shining like a beacon. She felt the slightest throb of pain in her temple. It had to be the unreasonable heat. She wasn't used to it.

'Ha ha, nice joke,' Kinza said. Her makeup had already melted away, but it left her face dewy and glow-y while Kashish was sure that she looked like a sweaty mess. They had just entered the house, when she realised Kinza had fallen back, talking to another family. Then she heard her name being called out and with a sigh, she walked up to the other family. This was how the night would go—her sister was going to introduce her to everyone, and she would have to smile politely and behave like she had just one or two brain cells.

Two guys walked away swiftly as she approached the two women. There was an older woman in a cream-coloured saree, while the other was a little older than Kinza and looked harried as her eyes followed the guys who had left.

After the introductions, they all went inside, and were soon herded into the ladies' section. A part of her had wondered if Kinza would tell everyone that she was an internet celebrity, but Kinza had completely forgotten about Kashish's social media superpowers as she went flitting from one group to another like a pale pink butterfly. Kabir trailed after his mother and Kainaat sat next to Kashish, watching everyone.

Kashish looked around. She could mine all of this for content! All these women vapidly talking about their jewellery and what their husbands had bought for them, the kids running around shrieking, everyone speculating on how much jewellery the bride would be given. Like *they* had some personal stake in it. It was so baffling.

A pretty girl in a turquoise shalwar kameez came running and sat down next to the old woman she'd been introduced to earlier.

'Ammajan!' she squealed, hugging the old lady who framed her face and kissed her forehead. Kashish felt that familiar twinge in her chest. These days it seemed to happen a lot more than it used to.

'Fiza, meri bacchi, how are you?'

The girl had long, straight hair, clear skin, and her eyes were an intriguing shade of grey. She was slender and simply stunning. Kashish found herself straightening her back, feeling appalled at how dowdy she felt in comparison.

Kinza had been right. She felt underdressed, all of a sudden. The girl was wearing pretty chandelier earrings that swung as she talked to her grandmother. Kashish stared, and the girl's eyes met hers. Quickly, Kashish looked away. But the girl was now walking up to her.

'Oh my god. Is it really you?' she whispered.

Kashish turned to her, a little pleased, a little mortified.

'I'm sorry?'

'You're Kashish Asif,' the girl whispered again as if she were talking about nuclear secrets. Kashish nodded.

The girl clapped her hands on her pink cheeks. 'Oh my god. I am such a huge fan. And my cousin! He's here. I have to call him and tell him. Oh my god, wait. He will be mortified. I saw what you did to him and I think...no wait...that's his mom there...and aaaaaa...I can't believe this...can we take a selfie?'

Kashish didn't understand anything, but she felt vaguely reassured that someone had recognised her finally and having one million followers had not proved to be a complete waste.

'Sure,' Kashish said.

The girl was so excited, she pulled out her mobile phone and angled it above them. They both smiled automatically, and Kashish turned to her.

'Um, you are?'

'Oh my god, I'm sorry I forgot to introduce myself! You're like so much prettier off camera but you look *amazing* on camera too. Is it the *lights*? Do you use any special makeup? I really, no wait, ah yes, I forgot. My name is Fiza,' she said.

Kashish smiled, trying to keep track of everything the girl was saying. 'Hi Fiza.'

'And this is my cousin's haldi. Oh my god, she's going to be so excited when she hears that you attended? How did you come? I mean, please don't take this the wrong way but who invited you?'

Kashish obviously took it the wrong way and her face flushed with embarrassment. 'I'm here with my sister,' she said quietly, indicating Kinza with her head.

'Aaaaaaa,' Fiza let out a tiny scream, startling Kashish and the other ladies nearby. 'You're Kinza Bhabhi's sister? Aaaaaaa. Why didn't she tell us all this while?'

Kashish looked around embarrassed, just as Kinza joined them. 'Fiza, what happened? You okay?'

'No, I'm not *okay*. Why didn't you tell me that your sister is Kashish Asif?' Fiza yelped. 'I can't believe this!'

Kinza frowned. 'Why? What happened?'

'Bhabhi! She's an internet celebrity! So many of us here are her *fans*. And oh…' her mouth turned into an 'O'. 'My cousin is here. She has to meet him.'

'Why?' Kinza asked, confused. 'Why does she have to meet him?'

'Because…' Fiza looked at her, as if trying to ask Kashish for help but Kashish didn't know what she meant. Was this cousin her fan?

'Um, because the idiot did something stupid and Kashish, um, she schooled him nicely and…'

Kinza felt her blood turn cold and then warm, almost instantly. Wait a minute. Sameer was *here*? *That* Sameer? He was Fiza's cousin?

'What? How come I didn't know about this, Munni?' Kinza asked, sitting down beside them. Kashish licked her lips nervously.

'It's nothing. It's part of the whole...where are you going?' she asked, her voice rising in nervousness, as Fiza leapt up and walked rapidly towards the main hall.

'To call him, so you guys can talk,' Fiza replied over her shoulder as she walked away.

Sameer Ehsan was here! And she was going to talk to him in less than a minute! She wasn't sure if she should stick around or run away. Worse, how was she going to explain anything to Kinza, who was looking at her curiously?

17

It was hard not to bring out one's phone during these functions but Sameer had always been the best-behaved boy, refusing to be fixated on his phone whenever he was surrounded by adults. He had chastised Sadeem so many times, for playing Free Fire with his friends while at family gatherings, even though he had been tempted to join the game himself.

But now, he slid out his phone from his pocket and glanced at Instagram, his fingers tapping on the screen until it took him to Kashish's profile. He checked her stories—there were some random photos of the sky, of balconies, of terraces, but no indication that she was in Chennai. She hadn't posted a new reel in a while, which in itself was surprising because she normally posted one every other day.

His eyebrows drew together as he tried to recall who she had been with. His mother had called out to someone called Kinza. He had no idea who that was. Of course his mother knew more people than he ever could.

The preparations for the haldi continued. He felt extraneous, sitting there, doing nothing. A part of him clamoured to get up and offer to help but he was also wary of being called a chamcha by his cousins or his brother, who would think he was mad for actually wanting to work.

His finger accidentally tapped on the video of Kashish where she'd dressed like him and made fun of his atta kneading skills and he winced, but thankfully the volume was muted. He watched her face as she replicated the way he'd shot his video, and he had to admit it was pretty funny, even though she'd lampooned him.

His brother glanced at his screen and rolled his eyes, even as Sameer quickly put away his phone.

'Go to the women's side with some excuse, bro. See if you can spot her,' he suggested.

Sameer looked at him like he was crazy. But then he saw Fiza waving at him, only her head and hand peeking out from behind the wooden screen. Frowning, he looked around. Was she waving at *him*?

'Um, Fiza didi is waving at you,' Sadeem informed him.

Shit. Why?

He got up slowly and Sadeem also followed suit. No one paid them any attention as they made their way there. Fiza's eyes were bright with excitement.

'Hey, um, what's up?' he asked.

'Oh my god, why didn't you tell me Kashish Asif is here!' she said in a loud whisper, reaching out to clutch his wrist.

'How would I even know she's here?' he asked, his heart in his throat. He swallowed. 'I mean…'

'No because of your little enmity thing on Instagram!' she said.

'You know about that?' he asked, eyes wide. 'You follow me?'

Fiza gave him an exasperated look. '*Of course* I do. And it was a *genius* move, bringing in Ammajan in your videos. But I've been following Kashish longer and I'm a *huge* fan. Oh my god, I can't believe she's here!' she said with a whisper that was more a suppressed shriek. Her eyes were bright and she looked like she was one second away from hopping like a bunny on steroids.

Sadeem looked at him shrewdly.

'Anyway, I came to get you,' she said, her hands tugging him behind the screen.

'What? Why?' he asked, his normally deep voice sounding like it had when he was fourteen. Behind him, Sadeem nudged him and whispered 'shut up'.

Fiza didn't seem to be bothered as she dragged him away to the women's section. Some of the women stared at him when he entered, followed by Sadeem. But he couldn't really take in anything because his eyes were fixed only on Kashish who was seated on a chair, staring at him.

Oh god. This was really happening. What was Fiza thinking? What would everyone else think? Then, instead of leading him to Kashish, Fiza turned and dragged him towards the little patch of garden at the back of the house. Er...what...

'Wait here,' she informed him succinctly before disappearing back inside the house.

Sadeem scratched his head. 'What is she doing?'

Sameer's jaw tightened with anxiety. His stomach churned. He looked down at himself, and then lifted his eyes to his brother who looked amused.

'You look good, bro,' he assured him.

'I don't really care but…' he trailed off. He did care. So much that his stomach kept clenching and unclenching and he felt something tickling at the back of his throat. But before he could say anything else, the door opened and Fiza was leading Kashish towards him.

This was freaking unreal.

Kashish looked bemused as she walked down the tiny steps. Sameer watched her, hoping he was not going slack jawed. His racing heart kept trying to see how much more it could take. He took in a deep breath to calm himself. Was Kashish pissed at him or at Fiza?

'Sameer, this is Kashish as you very well know,' Fiza said, her voice rich with amusement, as she reached him, one hand holding Kashish, as if she might run away. 'And Kashish, this is Sameer.'

The four of them stood in silence, broken only by Fiza's giggle. 'This is so *silly*. Of course you guys know each other.'

Sadeem, of course, decided to act like a proper idiot. 'I'm sorry, who?' he asked.

Fiza rolled her eyes. 'Hey, don't act like you don't know who she is,' she said.

Kashish gave him an appraising look but didn't say anything. This was so awkward. Sadeem laughed sheepishly. 'Okay fine. I'm sorry for pretending. I'm a huge fan, by the way. And so is my brother.'

Sameer didn't look at his brother but he hoped Sadeem knew that he was going to get his comeuppance for doing this. At the same time, he also wished he could be as easy and casual as his brother. Right now, it felt like he'd swallowed a handful of pebbles and couldn't speak around them.

'A fan?' Kashish asked finally, lifting an eyebrow elegantly. Effortlessly.

He didn't know what possessed him then. All the weird dreams, all the ways he'd thought he'd win her over by being witty and funny (Why? He had no idea), all the mental prep he'd been doing if ever she DM'd him back—everything seemed to have evaporated. What came out of his mouth made him want to hit himself over the head with his own boot.

'Well, not really. And I'm still not big enough to be considered a rival. But give me some time and I'll get there.'

18

Kashish's heart pounded as Fiza dragged her away from the main party. Thank god Kinza had been called away. And why was she being such a doormat? But the truth was, she was curious.

Sameer was so tall and even more good-looking in person. Her mind's eye catalogued everything about him as rapidly as it could. Broad shoulders, a hint of muscle beneath that good boy shirt, clean cut hair style, and those eyes. She'd noticed more than a few aunties looking at him appreciatively when he had walked into the women's side.

Her traitorous heart was doing all sorts of acrobatics but she stood her ground even as Fiza kept chattering about how it was amazing that Kashish was here.

'Why didn't you post anything about being here in Chennai?' Fiza said as she led her to a door.

Sameer was *behind* that door.

Shit.

It appeared that Fiza wasn't expecting an answer from her because she went on talking. 'I guess you want to keep some aspects of your life private, but oh my god, you will be mobbed if you come to my college. SO many of us are your fans! I love your reels! They're such fun!'

The words embarrassed her. She was no one. Just a girl who posted silly videos on Instagram. But she didn't say anything because she knew she was being unfair to herself and her team. They worked bloody hard at making her page consistent, even though she went off the rails sometimes with her own personal rants against clean-cut, good boys who were trying too hard to look sexy.

He didn't have to try too hard now, Kashish thought as she looked at him, standing in the patch of garden with another boy who looked like his brother. Something inside her melted and reformed rapidly. She was never tongue-tied around boys, but this was someone she had made fun of, someone who had gotten back at her, someone she'd schooled. It made it all the more weird for her to feel so... so vulnerable around him.

He was really, really good-looking.

Then of course, he had to speak and ruin it all.

'Let me know if I can help you in that,' she replied with a fake-sweet smile. 'I'm always happy to help out small businesses. You know, giving back to the community and all that.'

The other boy standing next to him snorted. And then he burst out laughing, even as Sameer flashed him an irritated look. Fiza was staring at the two of them, wide-eyed.

'Oh my god, are you guys playing out the whole enemy thing for real? Should I record? Can I put it on *my* Instagram?' she squealed.

'No!'

Kashish turned to Sameer, surprised that the two of them had shouted out the word together.

At this, Fiza grinned and covered her mouth. 'Oh my god, this is so funny.'

Kashish was tempted to ask her why she used 'Oh my god' so much but she kept quiet. Sameer looked embarrassed.

He cleared his throat. 'Um…I…that didn't come out the way I meant it to,' he said.

She looked at him appraisingly. 'Which part? The not a fan part?' The other boy shook his head slightly, a mischievous look in his eyes.

'All of it,' he said. Some of his confidence had disappeared and Kashish momentarily wondered if it was because of her. But he took a deep breath. 'Let's try this again.' To her surprise, he offered his hand.

She looked down at it warily, aware of the audience they had. Fiza was probably screaming 'oh my god' in her head.

Biting down on her lower lip, she took his hand. Her mind noted how dry and firm it was. Callused, and even a little rough. The contrast and friction against her own softer palm felt delicious. Now her own mind was screaming 'oh my god' for no reason whatsoever.

Sameer met her eyes and held them. 'I'm sorry for the way I acted. I'm sorry for the silly video I made. I'm sorry for unknowingly promoting domestic violence. And I'm sorry if I hurt you.'

Her heart pounded loudly, painfully. Her eyes were glued to his. She couldn't look away. Her surroundings melted away. She really hoped she wasn't wheezing because she felt like she was.

'And,' he continued, still holding her hand in the world's longest, strangest, fizziest handshake ever. He exhaled softly. 'I'm a huge fan.'

19

Sameer was a little gratified at the way her eyes widened at his words. Thankfully, it was enough to detract him from thinking about how incredibly soft her hand felt in his. He was grateful that she hadn't pulled her hand back immediately.

All too soon, the bubble popped, thanks to Fiza. She clapped loudly in delight, startling both of them. They withdrew their hands. His entire right arm prickled and he fought the urge to rub it aggressively.

She looked different from the way she normally did in her Instagram videos. He tried not to stare as he took in the black and red outfit she was wearing, the kurta flaring at the bottom slightly. Her dupatta was slung on her shoulders carelessly, and she was wearing some of sort of oxidised jewellery.

Fiza, in comparison, looked like an iridescent beetle—one who had accidentally tripped and fallen into a vat of blue paint.

'The two of you should *totally* do a collab!' she said, stepping forward to put a hand each on their shoulders.

'Fiza, shut up,' he said softly, embarrassed at his cousin.

'Why?'

He was going to have to explain it to her without an audience, that the last thing Kashish would want was to collaborate with him.

To his intense surprise and even shock, Kashish looked at him and spoke. 'Have your assistant reach out to mine and maybe we can work something out,' she said.

She had an *assistant*? Someone who was not a sibling?

Fiza clapped again, delighted at her machinations. Sadeem cleared his throat and stepped forward, offering *his* hand to Kashish.

'That would be me,' he said, trying to make his voice sound deep and cultured. He almost succeeded but sadly for him, Kashish didn't even look at his hand.

'Great. I'll connect you to my assistant and let's see if something works out,' she said, then turned around and walked away.

Don't go just yet!

Sameer wanted to call out to her, to make her stop, but he held back, not wanting to make a further fool of himself. She was already inside the house. How long was she in Chennai for? What did she mean by 'something working out?'

Sadeem dropped his hand, not even the least bit embarrassed.

'Whoa! Wow. I cannot believe this!' he whispered, his eyes wide.

'I know, right!' Fiza said, her voice almost gurgling in excitement.

'Why are you guys acting like this?' Sameer asked, annoyed.

Fiza and Sadeem exchanged a look.

'Listen, you idiot. If you do a collab with her then think of the viewership you'll have! The number of people who might discover you and follow you?' Sadeem whispered.

But none of that mattered to Sameer at the moment. All he was thinking of was how he could spend time with her, actively. When? How?

'Wait, what did she mean she'll connect you to her assistant?' he asked Sadeem, who shook his head and shrugged.

'Do we go inside and talk to her and ask her what she meant?' he asked.

Fiza grinned. 'Look at you, all eager to head into the ladies' section,' she rolled her eyes. 'I'll get the contact details for you. And I'll get you connected on WhatsApp as well.'

His heart thudded. 'Really? You'd do that?'

Fiza and Sadeem shared a look. 'Look at him,' Fiza whispered. 'I've never seen him like this.'

'Me neither,' Sadeem whispered. But then he rubbed his palms together in excitement. 'I wonder if her assistant is also a chick. If she's as beautiful as she is and…'

Fiza put her hands on her hips and quelled him with a look and Sadeem stopped blabbering.

'Why would you get her number for me?' Sameer asked, again. His eyes were still trained on the door behind which she'd disappeared.

'Because you seem smitten by her and I want to help,' she offered.

He looked at Fiza, startled.

Smitten? Him? No, but…how would it even work? She didn't seem affected by him at all. And she was a very popular Instagrammer already. He stood no chance. He was a tiny fly when compared to…

'He's probably telling himself why this is a bad idea,' Sadeem said. 'But you go ahead Fiza didi. Get us her number. Get the assistant's number. Maybe we can come up with a script for the two of them. Or wait! We can invite her home and shoot a cooking video with *her*!'

Sameer felt like he'd fallen face down on mud. This was going too fast. From collaborating to inviting her home to shooting a video *with* her, he was now wishing he hadn't acted like he was cool and unaffected. What would he say to her? Even if he did get her phone number?

'Yes yes! She lives in Bangalore and she's staying in Chennai with her sister for a few days. We'd better hurry and get something happening!' saying this Fiza flounced into the house.

'This is really great! If this works out, you'd better buy Fiza didi something she wants, because if not for her, none of this would have happened.'

Thank god Sameer didn't say anything like 'it's too early for all that to happen, you bozo,' because apparently, Sadeem was talking about the collaboration.

For now.

20

Kashish made it back inside the house, hoping no one would notice that her hands were trembling slightly. She was not sure what had happened out there exactly, but the way Sameer had looked when he said he was a fan, or the reaction her body had on shaking his hand was something she needed to understand on her own.

Or with Rania.

She pulled out her phone and shot off a text to her best friend.

He's here

Who?

Sameer

Sameer who

Eyeroll emoji That Sameer. From Instagram.

Wut? How?

I came for a wedding and he's here

Oooh and?

Kashish looked up and licked her lips nervously. This couldn't be done on text. Not when there were people looking at her inquisitively. She tapped a reply, telling Rania she would call her when she got back home. Rania sent her a sulking face emoji. Kashish put her phone away, her gaze catching on to the old lady she'd seen earlier.

For some reason, all her irritation with Sameer had fled, and she was left with a kind of trepidation. His cousin Fiza had seemed nice enough and not pissed at *her*. But what if others didn't feel this way? What if his grandmother gave her an earful?

She wanted to leave right away. She wanted to stay. She didn't know what she wanted any longer. Should she have lingered outside, talking to Sameer, instead of making a big show of walking back inside? It would have been nice to hang around outside, and maybe just look at him when he wasn't looking at her.

Sheesh.

She needed to get a grip. She couldn't be bowled over by his good looks. But try as she might, she couldn't recall what it had been about him that had annoyed her so much the first time.

Thankfully, she was put out of her own thoughts when Fiza joined her.

'Kashish! Come with me. I'll introduce you to the bride and also, while we're at it, I need your number and your assistant's number,' she said, looking serious.

'Oh. Um, sure. Why do you need my number?' she asked.

Fiza narrowed her eyes. 'You were serious back there about that collab, right?'

Kashish nodded.

Fiza smiled widely, her teeth gleaming. 'You don't mind, right? It's going to be such fun! So exciting! How can we coordinate if we don't have your number? I'm sure Insta DM is not easy to manage.'

That much was true. So, with a nod and tiny flutter in her belly, Kashish recited her number while Fiza saved it in her phone. Then she texted her on WhatsApp and then sent her another number.

'What's this?' Kashish looked up.

'Sameer's number. It's better you two are connected on WhatsApp,' Fiza said, her eyes back on her phone. She looked up at Kashish. 'I feel like I bulldozed you into this. You don't mind, right?'

Kashish stared back at her. 'It's a little too late for that, isn't it?'

Fiza stared back. Then she grinned. 'Sorry, but I just couldn't resist it. You should have seen the look on his face when I dragged him out of the men's section so the two of you could meet.'

For some reason, Kashish realised she was blushing. She pulled herself together.

'Okay. Cool,' she said, feeling anything but cool inside. She sent her Jessie's number.

'That's my assistant.'

'Okay, great,' Fiza put her phone away in the tiny purse that was slung across her body. 'Now, time to meet the bride.'

Half an hour later, Kashish belatedly realised that she was having fun, as she and some other girls sat with the bride and talked. Anisa looked radiant, dressed in a peach ghagra instead of the standard yellow outfit. It turned out, they all knew who she was, but no one made her uncomfortable and she posed for selfies with them, all the while feeling like a fraud. But soon, she was no longer *the* Kashish Asif. She was just another girl having fun, discussing the latest K dramas.

'Ooh look! The boys' side have come!' someone squealed, as she stood near the window.

'Shush! They'll all look up. Has the boy come too?' Fiza asked, as she scrambled to reach the window.

Anisa and Kashish exchanged a look, but there was also a slight pink tinge to her cheeks.

'Yeah, he's coming,' she said softly.

Kashish's eyebrows flew up. 'He told you?' she asked quietly, while the other girls clamoured near the window.

Anisa glanced at the window and gave a slight nod. Kashish grinned.

'Who is *that*?'

'Who? Who?'

'Oh my god, he's so cute.'

Fiza stood with her hands on her hips. 'That is my cousin Sameer,' she said.

Kashish's heart pinged in her chest on hearing his name. It urged her to get up and casually walk to the window and look down. Should she, too, look at Sameer from this window, like she was an eighteenth-century heroine?

But her brain firmly told her, nothing doing. Just stay put. And she listened for once, though her legs twitched.

Fiza was telling the other girls to stop salivating over him. Why? Did Fiza have her eyes set on him? Ugh. They were *cousins*. So? That sort of stuff still happened, but what did she care?

'Um, Kashish?' Anisa said quietly.

'Yeah?' Kashish looked at her, having almost forgotten that she was there.

'Go and look. It's okay.'

21

Sameer did get another glimpse of Kashish later that night and he held on to that moment because she was looking at him too. He was quite sure something wordless was passing between them and his heart thudded almost painfully. When the boys' side reached, suddenly they needed more chairs in the women's section, so he and Sadeem had pitched in, carrying chairs and arranging them.

His eyes had darted around, hoping to catch a glimpse of black and red in the sea of pastels and bling, and at first, he couldn't spot her. Disappointed, he went back to get more chairs when he spotted her, trailing behind the bride who was being led onto a makeshift stage.

She seemed a bit lost, as if she was looking for someone, too. Surely, not him. Her gaze swept across the crowd of women and he realised she was probably looking for her sister. He noted the expression of relief on her when she spotted her. Then she saw him.

They both froze. He should have straightened up and moved back to the men's section where he belonged but he couldn't, until his brother nudged him.

'Stop it,' he whispered harshly.

Sameer arranged the chair extra carefully and then walked away, feeling like his back was on fire.

Sadly, after that, there was no way he could spot her. He couldn't keep going into the women's section. And dinner was served in the larger lawn in front of house for the men while it had been arranged inside for the women.

Somehow, the evening had taken an almost magical turn for him. To think that he'd considered not attending! He would have missed out on seeing her, meeting her and now…he stared at his phone in disbelief. He had her number.

Fiza had sent it to him, along with another number, saying that it was Kashish's assistant's number and to seriously set up a collab and to stop mooning around like an idiot. Was it that evident, he thought, blushing.

Abbu had joined them just in time for dinner, and he had already started glancing at his watch repeatedly. It was 11 p.m. and still early when it came to haldi events.

'The two of us should go home. Sadeem can bring your mom and Ammajan back,' he suggested.

What? No.

'Sadeem doesn't have a driver's license yet,' he pointed out. Abbu rolled his eyes and let out a sigh.

'He doesn't look like a kid in any case. No cop will stop him,' he said.

'Abbu, that's not what you taught us,' Sameer protested, feeling a little annoyed at his father. 'You can't break rules according to your convenience. And he's not even that great a driver. Why would you send Ammi and Ammajan with him because *you* want to go home early?'

Abbu looked disgruntled. 'Fine. Ask him if he will come with me.'

Sameer wanted to tell him that he could go on alone, instead of waiting for one of them when to his surprise, Ammi called out to him. Ammajan wasn't feeling too well and they were all leaving.

Disappointment warred with worry and anxiety.

'What happened?' he asked, looking over Ammi's shoulder. He couldn't see Ammajan.

'Nothing to get worried about but I think she's got heartburn and she's saying she's fine but I know she isn't. We should leave in any case.'

'Thank god,' Abbu muttered. Sameer gave him a narrow-eyed glance.

Mutinously, he led Ammajan out of the ladies' section. She seemed a little annoyed at his attention, and kept batting his hand away.

'I'm not that old also. I can walk on my own,' she grumbled. Sameer didn't look up or around. His attention was entirely on his grandmother.

Fiza was leading her on the other side. 'I told her *not* to eat that chilli chicken. It was slathered in green chillies,' she hissed. Ammajan glowered at her.

'I took care of you two idiots, wiping your noses and your bums when your mothers needed a break, and now you two turn on me like this?' she asked, pulling her arm away from Fiza.

'That's why you shouldn't be so fixated on the older kids only,' Sadeem piped up. Ammajan glowered at him too, giving him the facial equivalent of the middle finger.

'Text me when you guys reach home and how she's doing,' Fiza said.

'Yeah. Sure.' Should he ask her if it would be okay to text Kashish? But then he saw the look of impatience on his father's face and the discomfort on Ammajan's face and bit back the question.

They reached home soon enough. His mind was ticking with ideas for the collab. He would have to tell his grandmother about Kashish, and he dreaded it. Ammajan would ask tons of inappropriate questions, make jokes about farting and bum pinching, and read more into whatever was happening. Which was? Nothing. Nothing, he told himself quickly.

Also, he was counting his chickens or eggs or whatever that analogy was. Kashish may not be interested in a collab with him after all. She could have just said that to get them off her back. She could have given Fiza her number just to shut her up.

As they changed out of their clothes, and got ready for bed, Sameer went into the guest room to check in on Ammajan.

She was removing fat gold studs from her ears, wincing a little as she tugged them out.

'I'm fine. Nothing a few farts won't get rid of,' she muttered. He made a face.

'I'll whip up some buttermilk for you. It might ease that heartburn,' he said. She looked at him and smiled.

When he brought the glass to her, the house was silent, except for the odd creaks and groans every now and then.

His mind had hopped on to the following day. If Kashish had come for the haldi, surely she would attend the nikah too.

'Sit here for a bit,' Ammajan ordered. He complied, even though he was itching to go back to his room and check his phone. Maybe Kashish would have messaged him.

Ha. That would be the day.

'Now tell me who this girl is, who has you so tied up in knots?' Ammajan asked, twisting his ear ever so slightly.

22

For Kashish the ride back was blessedly silent except for Kinza and Kaif Bhai talking softly to each other in the front. Kashish sat with the sleeping kids, her arm around Kabir so he wouldn't slip down while Kainaat's head was in her lap.

They passed by the beach and in the distance, white caps of the waves crashed against the shore. The dimly lit beach held a magical promise for her. She stared into the sky, at the moon hanging over the dark water, bobbing along with them.

She was going to have to come here during the day and it would have nothing to do with making Instagram reels. She wanted this for herself. In fact, this entire trip had been about herself, she thought with a certain amount of reluctance. She hadn't yet reached out to the café Jessie had found for her. And then there was Sameer.

Her heart gave a little bumpity bump when she thought of the way he'd looked when he held her hand and said he was a fan. Would he reach out to her first? Well, obviously. He was the one who wanted to collaborate, right? So why would she text him first? But her hand itched for some reason and she pulled up his contact on WhatsApp. The smile grew on her face when she saw that his DP was of him bending down to hug his grandmother from behind, his elbow around her neck, while she reached up and twisted his ear.

It was an affectionate photo, one that spoke of their love. Her forefinger hovered over the screen. She should say 'Hi'. No, she shouldn't. She needed to talk to Rania first before she decided to act like a fool over a boy. Knowing her friend, Rania would only tell her to go for it.

Something stopped her from doing it though. She looked at her sister and her husband, at her sister's half-turned profile, at the dimple on her cheek that added to her charm. She was smiling at something Kaif was saying and Kashish's heart ached for a reason she couldn't quite explain.

With barely any traffic at night to slow them down, they reached Kinza's home in record time.

'Whew. I'm so tired. And tomorrow is the wedding,' Kinza said as she removed her heels and shoved them inside the cupboard near the door. Kashish removed hers as well, groaning a little from the relief.

The kids had already gone upstairs with Kaif Bhai. It was just the two of them downstairs. The quiet house, the soft hum of the refrigerator in the kitchen, the louder hum of the AC in the children's bedroom switching on, all of this was making her feel very homesick all of a sudden. She missed Abbu acutely.

'What happened?' Kinza asked as she checked the kitchen and kept any leftovers from lunch in the fridge.

'Nothing. Just missing Abbu,' Kashish admitted. Kinza's expression changed a little and Kashish wondered why. But she didn't say anything to her.

'Did you get too bored today?' Kinza asked.

Kashish shook her head. She'd been the opposite of bored today. 'No, I met this girl Fiza and…'

'Who was that boy?' Kinza asked, eyes wide. 'I kept meaning to ask you.'

Kashish licked her dry lips. 'Her cousin.'

'Why did he look so familiar?'

Kashish had no idea what to tell her sister. Then she remembered something. 'That video you were watching back in Bangalore? On YouTube? That was him!'

'Oh!' Kinza's eyes widened. 'I see!'

'How do you know them?' Kashish asked before she could stop herself.

'I don't know them. Or I'd have known who he was, right?'

Kashish remembered something else. 'You met his mother just as we were entering?'

Something seemed to click in Kinza's head. 'Oh! He's Misba Apa's son?' she asked. Kashish shrugged. Kinza went on. 'Right. I think when I last saw him he was around thirteen or fourteen. I had no idea he'd become such a dashing young man.'

Kashish's belly flipped at the reminder of the dashing young man. God, this was stupid. She had to talk to Rania who would hopefully talk some sense into her.

'Okay, I'm tired,' Kashish said, faking a yawn. She didn't want to talk more about Sameer with her sister.

'Go on,' Kinza said.

Kashish went up the stairs. Kaif Bhai had come out, after having changed into track pants and a T shirt. He smiled at her absently and she headed into her room. However, something made her stop for a moment and she looked out just in time to see Kinza at the top of the stairs.

Kashish slid back into the shadows of her room when she saw Kaif Bhai pull Kinza close, his arm around her waist. He was holding her tightly and she was looking up at him, her eyes half-closed, a faint smile on her face.

She shouldn't be looking at this. She should go back inside and give them privacy, she thought as Kaif Bhai bent his head and kissed Kinza.

Heart thudding, Kashish went inside her room, her face ablaze. This was as bad as watching her parents be romantic with each other. Yuck. Not that she remembered anything of the sort.

She sat on the edge of the bed and put her hand over her racing heart. She wasn't disgusted by what she'd seen. In fact, apart from the embarrassment, the emotion that she felt most was longing. She wanted this for herself, too. Eventually. One day.

Much later, after her sister had gone away to her bedroom, Kashish lay back on the bed, her head resting on the pillow as she stared at the ceiling. Was it stupid of her brain to wonder what it would be like to have experienced such a moment with Sameer?

Oh my god, so stupid. So very stupid.

That was why her heart gave a loud thump when her phone pinged and it was a message from him, saying 'Hi'.

23

'It's a good thing today is Saturday,' Sadeem remarked from his bed, the following morning.

'Why?' Sameer asked, not looking away from his phone.

'Imagine if you had to attend college with that moony expression on your face? You wouldn't have been able to concentrate on anything.'

Sameer threw his pillow in the direction of his brother who caught it deftly. But he didn't look away from the phone. He was watching one of Kashish's old videos, a GRWM one where she was getting ready for a day at college.

Jeans. A long-sleeved top. Some accessories. A close-up of her ear lobe as she fitted dangly earrings. A smile. Her feet. Sneakers. And finally, a zoomed-out image of her fully ready.

The video had 3 million likes.

Also, Fiza was right. He *was* smitten.

Last night, he hadn't expected her to reply when he had sent her a tentative 'Hi'. He had escaped Ammajan's inquisitive questions by making some excuse about needing to use the bathroom and run from there. When his phone lit up with a reply from her, he felt like he'd stopped breathing.

Now what? What should he tell her? He'd already apologised. He knew that their respective assistants would make plans for their collab. But what was *he* going to do? Wait until then?

It was nice meeting you

Hmm

Hmm? His eyebrows went up, not sure how to respond to that. Before he could stop himself, he'd sent another message.

Are you coming for the wedding today?

Probably

Ok see you then

He felt like an idiot for some reason, wearing his heart on his sleeves when she was considerably cooler towards him.

'Are you boys going to be in bed all day?' Ammi called out from outside. Sadeem groaned.

'It's a Saturday. It's a working day for *you*, Ammi. Not us.'

'Don't I know that,' she said, her voice coming closer as she opened the door and peered inside. She frowned. 'Get up. Brush your teeth. Shower. Come out and have breakfast. See if Ammajan needs anything. I'll be back home soon. We have to go for the wedding tonight. Don't forget.'

With that, she walked away briskly. Sadeem huffed out a breath.

'Fiza didi shared the assistant's number with me. How soon is too soon to reach out to her?' he asked him.

Sameer didn't reply. He sat up, feeling like his hair was on end. Kashish had texted him just now.

I'm going to the beach. Wanna come?

Whoa.

Now?

Yeah. Why?

He frowned, and checked the time. It was just past seven. It would get hot pretty soon. But he didn't want to sound like a know-it-all or someone who refused to go to the beach because it was hot.

Nothing. I'll come. Which beach are you going to?

Besantnagar

Ok, see u there

He put away his phone and got ready in record time. He grabbed his motorbike keys off the wall and strode out after spraying himself with cologne. Then he sprinted back inside to change his shirt because he'd sprayed way too much.

'Where do you think you're going?' Sadeem asked, bemused.

'Bessie,' he said.

Sadeem sat up. 'What? Why?'

Sameer debated telling his brother but then the blabbermouth might mention something to Ammajan and that would be it. But she would get to know during their collab right? And that he had a massive crush on Kashish? Yeah, well, never mind.

'Meeting a friend,' he said as he left the room, praying he wouldn't bump into Ammajan.

Sadeem followed him outside, his hair sticking up comically. 'The friend's name wouldn't happen to be Kashish Asif would it?' he called out.

Sameer glared at him as he picked up his helmet.

'Keep your voice down. We're just meeting to hash out some ideas for the collab,' he said.

'Then I should come too!' Sadeem said, moving forward.

'Next time,' Sameer said recklessly, not sure if there would be a next time. But there was no way he was letting this chance go. If Kashish reached there before him, (he had no idea where she was staying) and if she decided it was too hot and wanted to go back, he would be very annoyed. And disappointed.

He didn't bother waiting for Sadeem to reply. He hopped onto his motorbike and rode away. For a moment the thought struck him if she was pulling a fast one on him and she wouldn't be there. Was this a prank and she'd set up a camera to record his reaction? Another way to humiliate him and rack up her views by posting it on her Instagram?

It's okay, he told himself. It was worth it. But deep inside, there was something else that propelled him forward.

She was going to be there.

24

'I'll be fine. Really. Please,' Kashish insisted as she walked to the gate where her auto was waiting.

Kinza looked very displeased. She had been surprised to hear that Kashish wanted to go to the beach. She would have gladly accompanied her if the children didn't have school that day. Both of them had half a day, and Kashish was glad of that.

'If you wait for half an hour, I can send them off to school and come with you,' Kinza called out, slinging her dupatta over her head quickly as she stepped out in her housecoat.

'It's fine. I'll manage,' Kashish said as she reached the gate.

'But you don't know Tamil, Munni. This isn't like Bangalore. You can't talk in English or Hindi and get away with it here!'

Kashish bit down on her lip and rolled her eyes. 'I'll make do. I know Kannada, no? How different can the two languages be?'

Kinza put her hands on her hips and exhaled. 'Fine. But call me if there's any issue whatsoever. I wish you'd told me before. I would have planned something. But okay go on. And come back before it gets too hot.'

Relieved that her sister had finally let her go, Kashish got into the auto and scrolled through her chat with Sameer. She wondered where he lived and how soon he would be able to get to the beach.

Last night, she'd called Rania after the message from Sameer, and the two of them had stayed up late, discussing what his angle was.

'Maybe he just likes you,' Rania said.

Kashish snorted. 'Please. He said some mean things and the way he said he was my fan…' her belly flipped and she felt breathless enough to take a deep inhale. 'But I don't know. Like what if he's being so nice just to exact some sort of revenge?'

'Conspiracy theorist much?' Rania asked. Kashish could sense the eyeroll even though they weren't on a video call.

'I don't know,' Kashish admitted.

'Listen, you should get your assistants to talk and then come up with a couple of videos for this collab, which is an excellent idea by the way,' Rania said.

'For him. How does it help me?' Kashish asked.

Rania sighed. 'Even though many people thought your video was funny, the first one you did? There were people who thought you were being mean. And then after the statistics video, you came across as judgy and serious.'

'But…'

'Doing the collab video with him will be good for your image. It will show a glimpse of the real you to the world,' Rania said warmly.

Kashish was silent as she processed this. She didn't want the world to see the real her. There was too much anger and ugliness and inexplicable feelings that made no sense to her. She was happy portraying the carefully constructed image of Kashish Asif to the world. Why would she want everyone to see what she was really like underneath it all? In fact, one of the reasons she had even set up her Instagram account was to step away from the real her and be someone else for a little while.

But she didn't voice it to Rania because even though she was her closest friend, there were things that could not be said even to her.

Rania's words had remained in her head when she woke up this morning. She stood at the open window and breathed in the humid air and wanted to do this. She was really going to do it.

In the auto, a faint wind blew her hair about and she tracked the location on her phone. She wondered how Sameer was coming there and for a brief moment, she felt unprepared to meet him. Physically and mentally.

Why had she sent him that text? What if he got the wrong idea about her asking him to meet her there? Well, what was the right idea? She had called him there for some reason, right? When she sent him the text, she told herself it was because they would do better in the collab if they had some sort of understanding of each other.

Lies. She just wanted to spend time with him. That thought warmed her but she tried not to focus on it.

The air suddenly vibrated with a Tamil song and she jumped. The auto driver was playing a song on the radio.

Taking a deep breath to calm her nerves, she took in the city. There were other beaches but she'd read up about this area. The idea of living in a locality where you could take two turns and end up with a view of the beach fascinated her.

The 2004 tsunami had affected this area too, but that had been years ago, before she was even born. She'd only read about it when she was looking up beaches in Chennai. She lifted her phone and angling it carefully, took a few photos of the roads they passed by, the huge trees on the sidewalks, the lush greenery everywhere.

There was the beach. She got down, paid the Auto Anna, texted her sister that she had reached safely, and stared.

The sight of the grey water in the distance, with the sunlight glinting on the surface like so many diamonds held her in thrall. She'd worn a long skirt paired with a top and had borrowed one of Kinza's sandals for the beach. She walked towards the water and her feet sank into the warm sand. It felt gritty but also remarkable for some reason.

There were a few joggers on the beach, and a smattering of couples, sitting on small hillocks of sand in the distance. As she walked towards the water, almost as if drawn towards it by some invisible string, she spotted tiny red crabs darting away here and there.

Just before the edge of the water, she took off her sandals and strung them through her fingers. Her feet sank into the wet sand and she wasn't sure she liked the sensation so much. But she kept standing there, watching the waves rush towards her giddily.

Her toes curled into the sand, finding a foothold. In the distance, a boat bobbed in the water. She took photos and videos, all of which she planned to send to Jessie so she could compile them into a reel.

It was exhilarating. It was a heady rush. The wind flattened her skirt against her body, and the edges flapped about. As the water drew away from her feet, she laughed out aloud. For the first time in a long while, for no reason whatsoever, she was just glad to be happy, glad to be alive, and present in the moment.

She spread her arms and enjoyed the feel of the water hitting her ankles. Not so much the seaweed that scraped past but she jogged in place to remove that.

She should have come here sooner. She should have come here every day.

'Glad you're enjoying this so much.'

The deep voice made her turn suddenly and her ankle twisted, making her slip. Oh no! She was going to land in the wet sand! But before that could happen, a strong arm reached out and held her firmly. She looked into Sameer's chocolate brown eyes.

And of all the things to tell him, she ended up saying, 'I'm in love.'

25

Sameer nearly dropped her then but recovered in time and held on as she cleared her throat. 'I mean, I'm in love with the beach. It's so beautiful right now. I can't believe I hadn't come until today!'

He helped her stand up and let go, trying not to focus on the way his hands tingled. Her cheeks were flushed too and she looked away, tucking a strand of her hair behind her ear. He tried to take in the view of the water as it probably appeared to her but having grown up here, it wasn't quite the same for him.

'It's a pretty beach,' he admitted, just as his eyes spotted a gleaming turd. Wincing, he put his hand on her shoulder without much thought and steered her away from that disgusting sight.

She cleared her throat.

'Did I disrupt your plans?' she asked.

It was on the tip of his tongue to tell her he had no plans and he'd been busy going over her old photos and videos, but of course he couldn't tell her that. He'd sound like a stalker.

'It's fine,' he said. Now what? Now that he was here, standing beside her, what were they going to do?

'I thought we should discuss the collab,' she said.

He fought the tiny curl of disappointment. Of course she'd called him for that.

He nodded. 'Sure, what did you have in mind?'

She didn't say anything for a few moments and he turned to her. She was looking out at the water and he figured he could stare at her profile all day.

'Do you post only cooking videos?' she asked.

He blushed for some reason. 'Mostly, yes. I mean, it's a newish account. I was thinking of…'

He paused. Should he explain why he started doing this? He pursed his lips and turned to her. 'I wanted to make a repository of food knowledge, especially that which is passed down from our elders.'

Her eyes lit up. 'That's actually…' she exhaled. 'That's actually lovely. So why did you do that whole atta kneading thing?'

He couldn't stop himself from hitting his forehead with the palm of his hand. 'That was all Sadeem's idea. He thought I should make cooking look sexy. In my defence, I disagreed and I was very uncomfortable with the idea.'

She stared at him for a few beats and then grinned. 'Did it work?'

It got you to notice me!

He didn't voice the thought but he shrugged and kept his voice even. 'So this famous influencer decided to take me down a peg or two for some reason,' he said, grinning.

She rolled her eyes. 'I never apologised to you for that,' she said after a moment.

'There's no need to apologise,' he said.

'You were trying something new. And I made fun of you without a second thought. Sorry about that,' she was gazing up at him. Somewhere in the region of his navel, it felt like his stomach had just decided to go into a freefall.

'Isn't that par for the course for Instagram? Isn't that what a lot of creators do?' he asked. He'd been checking out Instagram more actively and he noticed that what she'd done was tame in comparison to some of the more severe take-down videos creators made about other creators.

She shrugged. 'Maybe. But I don't normally do that.'

So what was special about me?

If he'd been his brother, he would have blithely asked her. He really wished he was more like Sadeem.

'Anyway, that's in the past. What did you have in mind for this collab?'

She pursed her lips and didn't say anything at first. Then she spoke up. 'My friend thinks that it will let my audience see a glimpse of the real me.'

'And you don't agree?'

She looked like she wanted to say more but couldn't bring herself to say it, which was surprising, given how confident and sure she seemed in her videos. For a moment, he appreciated the chance to see her as she was, without a mobile screen between them. He didn't know what he'd done to deserve it.

'Maybe we could do a couple of videos of you showing me around your city?' she suggested.

He cocked his head. 'That's a good idea but how about we do one video each that shows our respective strengths.'

'What do you mean?' she asked, her eyebrows knitted.

'Your Aunty K videos are really hilarious,' he said. Her face closed up immediately and he wondered if he'd made a mistake somehow. Licking his lips, he went on, even though he struggled a bit to continue. 'Maybe we do a video of Aunty K with me? And you can do a cooking video with me and Ammajan?'

She was quiet for so long that he wondered if he'd really messed up. He would never understand women.

'That's actually a really good idea,' she said finally.

Pleased, he exhaled softly. He'd been so anxious that she would shoot down his idea…he stopped. Yes, he was smitten by her but he couldn't completely bury what made him the way he was. He had to be a little more assertive and less like a puppy dog waiting for scraps of affection.

'Great. Good that we're on the same page,' he said, clearing his throat. 'We could plan and shoot a video with my grandmother tomorrow if you have no other plans?'

She nodded.

'And Aunty K?' he pushed. Kashish's Aunty K videos had transformed her from a run-of-the mill influencer to something more and his head was playing around with a couple of scenarios already.

She looked away for a moment before her gaze came back to his. 'Sure. We can shoot that after we do your cooking video.'

He nodded, wondering why she looked so unhappy about it. But before he could say anything, the skies opened up and rain lashed down at them, drenching them in minutes.

26

Kashish wanted to take back the words as soon as she said them, but it started raining at that very moment. Both of them looked at each other, not sure what they should do. In the back of her mind, she knew she had to tell Sameer that maybe they shouldn't do an Aunty K video while she was in Chennai in her sister's home. Kinza would never understand.

The idea for Aunty K had come to her a couple of years ago when Kinza had come to Bangalore to stay with them during the holidays and the way she called Kaif Bhai numerous times a day, checked in on him, made sure he was eating even while she was in another city, irritated Kashish. Kinza wasn't with them entirely, even when she was right there with them physically. It made her wonder if all women were like this. Did they get so caught up in this persona of being a wife and mother that they completely forgot to be themselves?

Aunty K became a symbol of everything Kinza represented. A somewhat foolish woman entirely in love with her husband, making sure she kept her husband happy no matter what, not caring if others got hurt in the process. Kashish kept the videos short and snappy, shot them with utmost seriousness. To get into the Aunty K mode, she rifled through Kinza's spare wardrobe that she kept in Bangalore, chose the jazziest of outfits and pretended to cook while wearing them.

Most of the videos were exaggerated, but the engagement that Kashish got for the videos was beyond her expectations. Nothing she had ever done until this could match up. Aunty K turned things around for her, rapidly growing her numbers, reaching the magic million. She did other videos as well, visited cafés and bookstores and restaurants, but none was as successful as the Aunty K ones.

And now, swept up by the intensity of being with Sameer, she'd agreed to what he asked. Her sister might be absent-minded and lost in her own little world that comprised her husband and kids, but she was no fool and would figure out what was going on. It was a wonder she hadn't seen the Aunty K videos yet and cottoned on to what Kashish had done.

The rain pounded over them and wait a minute…he was holding her hand? Just to lead her away apparently, but it still sent a frisson of something through her arm. She didn't pull away.

'Where should we go?' she asked him over the downpour. There was no place for them to take any shelter. There had been no indication of rain and neither of them had an umbrella with them.

Sameer looked around wildly. In seconds, it seemed as if the beach had emptied. It was surreal. 'We could go to my house,' he said.

'Is it close by?'

He nodded. 'I came on my motorbike. We can go home and dry off,' he suggested.

She looked down at her sodden skirt and felt extremely self-conscious. What would his parents think? But he was already leading her away from the water towards the road. The rain continued battering them and despite everything, Kashish felt acutely alive in the moment. She looked over at him, tall and serious. She had to stop herself from doing something silly. Like pulling him down towards her and laying a smacking kiss on his lips.

Her face heated and every inch of her palm that was in his, felt like it was on fire. They reached the road and he led them to where all the motorbikes were parked. The rain had lessened in intensity but it was still pouring down.

'Can you ride in the rain?' she asked him.

He nodded. 'I'll manage.'

'Or should we wait it out somewhere?'

'Where?'

They both looked around. The various lanes that led into the bungalows and houses were all lined with trees.

'Aren't there any coffee shops around?' she asked. There should be, right? This was a perfect spot for a venture like that, looking out over the swirling grey waters.

He shrugged. 'Probably. I don't know?'

She didn't want to go to his home looking like a drowned rat. He straddled his motorbike and she sat behind him gingerly, feeling some of the exhilaration slide away, to be replaced by a growing sense of misery because of the rain. Her clothes were sticking to her but then, they were also sticking to him. And his back was broad and… she looked away, not sure how to process all that she was feeling inside.

This was a physical attraction. Of course. He felt it too. So why did it feel momentous? Why did it feel like she was on the cusp of something big?

As Sameer drove away from the beach, she looked back at it with an acute sense of loss that she couldn't quite understand. Her feet were sticky with sand and there was an overall feeling of ickiness that probably came from the muggy air.

Her phone buzzed. Had to be Kinza. What would she tell her? That she was going to Sameer's home? What would Kinza say to that?

'We'll reach my house in ten minutes,' he called out to her over the pouring rain.

She didn't reply but slid her phone out of her sling bag and peered at the screen. Water droplets splashed on it immediately. It *had* been a call from Kinza. She covered the screen and quickly typed out a message saying that she was fine and taking shelter.

Sameer wove the motorbike between cars and other vehicles with such ease. The rain slowed down as they moved away from the beach and then it stopped.

She wiped the screen with her palm and looked at the messages her sister had left. She didn't read them. She would read them later when she was going back.

Sameer stopped the motorbike before a medium-sized grey house.

'We're here,' he said as she got down. He pushed the wet hair from his eyes.

'You didn't wear a helmet,' she remarked. He hadn't given her one either. Many people didn't wear helmets here. It wasn't like in Bangalore where you'd get fined if you were on a two-wheeler without one.

He shrugged, seemingly unaware, and then he strode towards the gate and opened it. 'Come on,' he said.

Was she an idiot to trust him? But Rania's words the previous night came back to her and maybe, just maybe, there were times in life she had to take things at face value and not look for hidden agendas.

27

Sameer wished he'd had the foresight or the time to tell Sadeem that he was bringing Kashish back home with him. Ammi wouldn't be at home but everyone else was. He hoped the living room wasn't too messy.

She walked through the gate, looking nervous and worried.

'Don't worry. My whole family is at home,' he said.

She looked stricken. 'What?'

'Yeah, I mean it's not like I'm taking you to an empty house where the two of us would be alone,' he said, feeling his face heat up. Shit. That came out wrong somehow and he gave a mental facepalm.

'I wasn't worried about that,' she said softly.

'Then?'

'What will your parents think? I look terrible!' she looked down at herself.

Last night, he'd been too stunned at her presence to notice the finer details about her, but now, even though her clothes were drenched and her hair lay in ropy curls around her shoulders, her skin was flushed and pink and he just wanted to keep looking.

'Is terrible a synonym for ethereal these days?' he asked, mentally patting himself on the back for having thought of something his brother was more likely to say.

'Are you not wearing your contacts or do you need to get your eyes checked?' she grinned. He grinned back.

'I'll have you know that I have perfect eyesight,' he said.

She clicked her tongue and gave him a quick onceover and rolled her eyes. 'Perfect is overrated.' But she still looked nervous. He decided to allay some of her worries.

'Come on inside. It's okay. No one will mind,' he said, even though he knew Ammajan would give him an earful, asking what was going on. If he wasn't careful, she would ask in front of Kashish.

He unlocked the main door and stepped in, half wishing the weather hadn't played spoilsport because they would have still been talking to each other at the beach if not for it. Maybe they would have found a relatively clean place to sit down and just talk without bothering about anyone else. Or he should have listened to her and taken her to a café. But he had wanted to bring her home. Some instinct told him to do this and now he wasn't sure if it was going to bite him in the ass.

Sadeem was in the living room watching TV. He looked up and did a double take when he saw Kashish walk in. Sameer mouthed 'behave' even as Sadeem jumped up.

'Hi! What's going on?' he asked.

'We were at the beach when it started raining,' she explained.

'And I suggested she come here,' Sameer added.

Sadeem lifted an eyebrow that spoke more than it ought to.

Abbu strode in from his bedroom holding on to this newspaper. 'What's going on?' he asked.

Sameer introduced Kashish. Thankfully Abbu was not the inquisitive sort and settled down to read the paper as if this was a normal occurrence.

'You can freshen up here,' he said, leading her to the common bathroom near Ammajan's room. She nodded and walked through. 'I'll get you some of Ammi's clothes to change into.'

'That won't be necessary,' she said quickly. 'These will dry off soon I'm sure.'

'Yes, but there's sand in it and it will all get very sticky and uncomfortable.'

'That's okay.'

'My mother isn't at home right now but she'll have my hide if she knows I didn't get you comfortable.'

Kashish went into the bathroom to freshen up, while Sameer ran to his parents' bedroom. Ammi was going to have his hide in either case. Should he call her and quickly check?

'What is going on?' Sadeem asked, standing at the door to the bedroom and peering inside.

'Thought I'd give her something of Ammi's because her clothes are all wet?' he said.

'I didn't ask about that. What is going on, bro? Why did you bring her home?' he whispered.

'We were both getting wet in the rain!' Sameer protested, pulling out his phone and dialling Ammi's number.

'I just reached office, and if you're calling to ask where…' Ammi's voice crackled down the phone, already prickly with annoyance.

'Can I give something of yours to a girl to wear?'

'What? Which girl?'

'I met her yesterday and then I went to the beach to meet her and we got wet in the rain so I brought her home.'

There was complete silence on the other end.

'Ammi?'

'I'm just wondering if I've slipped into an alternate dimension,' she remarked.

'Ha ha, very funny. I needn't have called you but I didn't want to give your clothes to her without asking you first.'

'Fine. Give her something comfortable to wear but who is she? What were you doing with her on the beach? And where did you meet her yesterday? And again, *who* is she?'

It was an odd, almost surreal moment for Sameer to have an epiphany and he couldn't do anything about it now. Not while his brother was listening in on the conversation. Not while Kashish was right outside, in the bathroom. Not while his mother was still waiting for his reply.

But this had become more than a crush.

28

Kashish clapped a hand on her mouth when she saw her reflection in the mirror in the bathroom. She hadn't realised she'd look like *this*—worse than a drowned rat, bedraggled, her hair like snakes.

Shit.

Sameer had seen her like this and said she looked ethereal. He had to be kidding. Or was he pulling a fast one on her?

She washed her hands in the wash basin and splashed some on her face. Then she used the water spray to rinse off the sand from her feet and even her calves.

There was a knock on the door and she jumped. She'd made a mess of the bathroom. She quickly used the water spray to hose off as much sand as she could from the bathroom floor.

'Kashish?'

Sameer sounded muffled.

'Yeah, one sec,' she said as she opened the bathroom door gingerly. He handed her a shalwar kameez.

The only way she was going to feel fresh was if she showered.

'Thanks but I'll go to Kinza Api's home and...'

'Get changed. Ammajan is making breakfast. You can eat and then I'll drop you to your sister's house,' he said.

She frowned, not liking his tone. She didn't like being told what to do. She shut the door on his face and leaned back against it. Why had she agreed to come here? She should have resisted. She should have stayed at the beach. They'd both gotten drenched anyway.

Now, she stared at the floral print shalwar kameez in her hand. Should she do this? Maybe she should just walk out and leave. She could book an auto and...she was overthinking this. Sameer was just being kind. She was uncomfortable in her clothes and it wasn't like he'd brought her to an empty house.

She looked longingly at the shower but it would be absolutely bonkers to shower in his house. Like this was any less bonkers.

She peeled the sodden clothes from her body and then, with a grimace, she donned the clothes he'd brought for her. They were two or three sizes large for her and hung on her body. She looked ridiculous. She pulled her hair back and twisted it in a bun at her nape.

If he was standing outside, waiting with a camera to film her and then post the video on his Instagram, she was going to have to murder him.

She stepped out warily, looking this way and that. There was no one.

Breathing a sigh of relief, she cleared her throat. Still no one. Maybe there was a hidden camera somewhere. If it had been her, she would most certainly have done it. But maybe, just maybe, Sameer wasn't as devious as she was.

She walked in the direction of the living room where Sameer's father was reading the newspaper. He didn't even look up. Voices floated in from the kitchen so she walked in the direction.

She stood at the door and took in the scene.

The old lady from last night was sitting at a kitchen island, deftly rolling out something white. Kashish couldn't understand what she was doing at first because it seemed like something long and white kept dropping off from her palms into the steel plate below.

Sadeem was at a counter, wiping his eyes and sniffling as he sliced onions. Sameer was nowhere in sight.

The old lady saw her first.

'Come, come,' she said. There was no smile on her face and Kashish didn't feel too welcome, but she stepped inside the kitchen anyway.

Sadeem turned around and smiled at her warmly. 'Come and sit down, Kashish,' he said, sniffling again.

'Bas kar drama,' the woman said, rolling her eyes.

'Drama?' Sadeem asked as he went back to the onions.

'Can I help?' Kashish asked. This was so awkward!

'He will manage. You help me with this,' the woman ordered.

'I don't know what this is, Aunty,' Kashish frowned, watching the woman rolling out what looked like elongated pasta between the palms of her oiled hands.

'No aunty. I'm Ammajan,' she said.

Kashish wasn't sure how to respond to that. She wasn't used to calling other people by their family monikers. Like she could never ever understand how Kinza could call Kaif Bhai's mother, Ammi.

Ammi was Ammi. Her Ammi. She would never call someone else's mother Ammi.

But maybe Ammajan was okay. She didn't have any living grandparents on either side of her family.

'Okay, so what is this, Ammajan?' she asked as she sat down near the woman.

'You've never eaten sutriyan?' Ammajan asked.

Even Sadeem turned around, surprised.

Kashish shook her head. 'No, I don't know what this is.'

Ammajan looked at her speculatively, but thankfully she didn't ask why her mother had never made it for her.

'Come, sit down. I'll show you. Here, you have to grease your palms like this,' and she handed her a transparent jar of oil.

Nervously, Kashish took it from her and smeared some oil between her palms.

'I'm done with the onions and here comes the chef. He can start the akhni,' Sadeem said, pushing away from the counter dramatically as Sameer entered the kitchen.

Apparently, he'd taken a quick shower or he'd forgotten to dry his hair after getting wet in the rain. Either way, she tried hard not to stare at him, dressed in a simple white T-shirt and sweatpants. He looked comfy while she was sure she looked demented. Without giving her a second glance he placed a large vessel on the stove and switched it on.

Kashish felt something she hadn't felt ever. She felt… lucky? What everyone saw on their screens, those videos of Sameer cooking, she was going to see it live. None of this was being recorded by anyone. She glanced around. No cameras. No smartphones.

This was…life.

Ammajan nudged her, expelling a long suffering sigh.

'Here. Look *here*.' And she handed her a bit of white dough. 'Look and learn.'

29

Sameer was extremely aware of Kashish sitting in his kitchen island, making sutriyan with Ammajan. It was so surreal, so unbelievable that he had to pinch himself a couple of times while he stirred the onions, to remind himself that this was really happening.

She was talking softly to Ammajan, asking her how sutriyan was made and he wondered how come she had never eaten it.

'Don't they make this in Bangalore?' he asked, looking at her finally. She looked ridiculously adorable, and even if the clothes were too loose for her, he couldn't bring himself to think that they belonged to Ammi.

She shrugged. 'I don't know. Maybe they do. Maybe they don't.'

He realised he knew very little about her except that her sister lived in Chennai. 'So, who else is in your family?' he asked.

He saw her shoulders stiffen a little and he turned back to the stove. The onions were getting browned. Time to add the adrak lehsun. He scooped out some in a spoon and added it, inhaling the sharp mingled flavours and turned back to her once again.

'Just me and my father,' she replied quietly.

Oh.

Ammajan who was showing her how to make sutriyan, stopped her from rolling one out too long. 'No, no, not that long. It has to fit between your palms, ma. Where's your mother?'

Sameer rolled his eyes as he added the mutton pieces to the pot. Ammajan was so inquisitive. As the mutton pieces seared, he winced a little because he knew Ammi was going to be mad that he'd used up the mutton she'd kept for Sunday lunch just because he wanted to impress Kashish with sutriyan for breakfast.

Kashish cleared her throat. Once, then twice.

'She passed away some years ago,' she said.

Sameer froze for a second and then turned around. Even Sadeem, who was now chopping the tomatoes, looked at her sympathetically. Kashish's face was stone-like. Impassive and yet, somehow irritated. She really didn't want to talk about her mother. But Ammajan was Ammajan.

'What happened?' she asked, as she took another ball of dough from the plate and started making smaller rounds with it.

'She fell sick and passed away,' Kashish's voice was so soft, her words weren't even audible.

Ammajan patted her back and nodded.

'I'm sorry,' Sameer said. Kashish didn't acknowledge him as she concentrated extra hard on making the sutriyan.

'Look, she's a natural. She's got it so quickly. Not like you two blockheads,' Ammajan said.

Sadeem groaned as he handed him the tomatoes. 'Ammajan, we're good at sutriyan too,' he protested.

'At eating it,' Ammajan grumbled. Kashish looked faintly pleased and even grinned a little. Sameer immediately felt tons lighter.

'Your sister will be fine with you having breakfast here with us, right?' he asked, thinking of it only now.

'I'll tell her in a bit,' Kashish said, once more concentrating on the sutriyan. 'This is like pasta, isn't it?'

'Pasta shasta,' Ammajan scoffed. 'Hmpf.'

Sameer's eyes met Kashish's for a second and they both shared a look of fond exasperation.

'Wait till you eat this. You'll forget all your pasta.'

'Aunty, I mean Ammajan, is this like regular breakfast food?' she asked, looking around them. 'It looks like a lot of work for breakfast.'

'Would you make biryani for breakfast?' Ammajan asked her. Sameer groaned inwardly.

'What? No. I don't even know how to make biryani,' Kashish muttered.

'That's okay. But if you knew how to make, would you make it for breakfast?' Ammajan asked.

Kashish shook her head. 'But we've had leftover biryani for breakfast sometimes. I mean, Abbu especially loves it. He says it tastes best like that.'

'Of course it does. He's right. But I don't think anyone makes biryani for breakfast, from scratch,' Ammajan remarked. Sameer felt the heat of their combined gazes on his back. He had to make an effort *not* to turn around.

'That means…'

'That's right. No one makes sutriyan for breakfast either.'

'Then…'

Ammajan gave another long suffering sigh. 'Someone here wants to impress you. That's why.'

Ammajan and her big mouth. Sameer was not going to turn around to look at them. Ever.

Instead, he stirred the mutton and added the red chilli powder and salt. The fragrance of the masalas rose in the air and he took the chopped coriander Sadeem handed to him. He knew Kashish was staring at him. He glanced back.

'Keep making, keep making,' Ammajan said, rolling her eyes and nudging Kashish's elbow.

'Yes, yes,' Kashish replied and went back to what she was doing. But Sameer couldn't quite explain what he felt in that moment. Never in his wildest dreams would he have thought that Kashish would be sitting at his kitchen table, make sutriyan with Ammajan and looking at him like that.

Like what? What was going on here?

He had no idea.

They had all the time in the world to find out. Or at least until she was in Chennai. And then? What would happen when she returned to Bangalore?

He'd worry about that later.

30

Kashish got down from the auto. It was just past noon.

Sameer had wanted to drop her back to Kinza's home but she insisted she could go back on her own. She was carrying a plastic bag with her wet clothes from the beach. A lot of explanations would need to be given.

Just the thought of it was exhausting but it had to be done. The door opened and Kinza stood there, looking at her with a raised eyebrow.

'Whose clothes are you wearing? Where were you? Why didn't you answer my calls? What the hell is going on?'

Groaning softly, Kashish walked past her inside the house.

'Kashish, I asked you a question! Several questions!' Kinza said, following her inside.

'Sorry, Api. I wanted to call you back but I got busy,' Kashish said.

'Busy doing what? How long does it take to send me one message? How can you be so careless!' Kinza asked, her hands on her hips.

'The kids aren't back yet?' Kashish looked around. It was odd that the kids had school today while Sameer and Sadeem were at home.

'Kashish! Answer my questions! Why are you being so secretive?'

Kashish turned to her sister, annoyed. 'I went to the beach. Sameer came there. It started raining so he took me to his house. His whole family was there and I had breakfast with them. He wanted to drop me back but I told him I could come back alone. That's it.'

Kinza stared at her in shock.

'What? Who is Sameer?' she asked in a whisper.

'The boy from the YouTube video,' Kashish replied.

'Misba Apa's son?' she asked with a frown.

Kashish shrugged. 'If that's his mom's name. I don't know. She wasn't at home but his grandmother and father and brother were there. They made sutriyan for me for breakfast,' she said.

Kinza was silent for a bit. She sat down on the sofa. 'But why was he at the beach? Why did you go to his house? You don't even know him!'

Why was Kinza upset that she'd gone to Sameer's home? It wasn't such a big deal, right?

'I told you, I met him last night. We're both Instagrammers. We…' she really didn't want to tell Kinza that she had called him there. 'What's the harm? His family was really sweet and they didn't mind that I crashed their Saturday morning.'

Kinza sighed. She rubbed her forehead in agitation. 'These sort of things aren't done, Munni.'

'What sort of things?'

'You're a girl of marriageable age. And he's a young man. You can't be seen travelling alone with him and going to his house like this? Whose clothes are you even wearing?'

Kashish's mouth fell open. 'Wait, rewind that a bit? A girl of *marriageable* age? I'm eighteen!'

'I know and no one is getting you married tomorrow but this sort of stuff looks bad for you and…'

'Then no family will want me anyway because of my Instagram account,' she said, feeling annoyed at her sister's assumptions. She still couldn't wrap her head around the marriageable part, even though she was aware that girls got married early in her community. She'd never thought herself to be on par with them. It was disconcerting to find herself being clubbed with other eighteen year olds, many of whom, she was sure, were certainly *not* waiting to get married.

'Why? What sort of things do you post there? Nothing shameful and indecent, no?' Kinza looked stricken.

Kashish didn't know what to tell her. 'Api, you're making a big deal out of nothing. Please. His family was fine about it. Why are you getting so worked up?'

'That's because he's a boy and you're a girl. This sort of stuff always affects the girl more than it does the boy.'

'Are you even listening to yourself?' Kashish asked. 'This is ridiculous.'

'Why are you wearing someone else's clothes?' Kinza asked, fixated on that for some reason.

'Oh for the love of God! They're his mother's clothes. Mine had got wet and dirty in the beach and he insisted I change into this so I could be more comfortable,' Kashish burst out. She'd anticipated Kinza getting a little angry that she hadn't answered the phone but she hadn't expected this level of grilling.

Kinza shook her head. 'I don't like this. You're being too familiar with that boy. This sort of thing isn't done. His family might have seemed okay but inside they'll be wondering what sort of family we come from that we let you gallivant around to some strange boy's home.'

Kashish had heard enough. She stood up.

'Well, when they arrange marriages for us girls, don't they essentially send us to some strange boy's home and expect us to live there forever?'

All the joy she'd felt from the morning had evaporated. She was tired, cranky, and she was in no mood to argue with her sister.

'Stop being contrary,' Kinza said.

'Then stop acting like you're my mother.'

The words had come out before she could stop herself, her tone harsher than she'd intended.

Kinza looked up at her, shocked. Kashish knew she should apologise but the words wouldn't come out of her mouth.

She was angry. She was hurt. All these years Kinza had never bothered to check what she was doing. How could she expect Kashish to treat her as a figure of authority all of a sudden, and *why*?

Kinza wasn't her mother, after all.

31

The atmosphere at home was tense. Kashish and Kinza weren't talking to each other and the children had cottoned on that something was seriously wrong. They didn't bother Kashish much, and she was grateful for that. She could not deal with their constant chatter right now.

She was on the phone, looking up train tickets to Bangalore. It was time she went back but something stopped her from doing it. Her finger hovered on the screen.

Going back right now would be childish. She didn't want to miss out on a chance of doing that collab with Sameer, just because of a silly fight with Kinza. But the fight had been *because* of him, right?

If she went back to Bangalore, then Kinza would have won. So if she was going to show her sister that she couldn't rule over her, then wouldn't it be better to stick around and do exactly what she wanted?

In the end she didn't buy the train ticket. But she was miffed. Things had been going so well on this trip. So what if she'd gone to his house? What was the big deal?

And what about the wedding tonight? Was Kinza going to leave her at home and go? That would be silly, right?

She really wanted to go for the wedding, only because she knew Sameer would be there.

She'd had fun in his house. The easy camaraderie between the brothers, the hilarious backhanded compliments and insults that Ammajan doled out, the sedate father who looked like he'd continue reading his newspaper even if he was dropped in the middle of a hurricane... Their mother was at work, but her absence didn't stick out. Not like Ammi's did.

She couldn't remember the last time she'd sat down for such a lavish breakfast with her father. Most mornings, she had cornflakes or quickly made a sandwich for herself before leaving for college. On weekends, Abbu made omelettes or French toast but that was it.

The rich taste of the sutriyan, so much like biryani but even better somehow, still lingered on her tongue. Ammajan had wanted her to take some for Kinza's home but she refused. She had already intruded on their morning. It was embarrassing enough.

When it was time for lunch, Kinza knocked on the door and pushed it open and walked in. Kashish was surprised to see her. She knew she'd hurt her sister but what she'd said was the truth, wasn't it? She was tired of pretending that they were like any other happy family.

'Come downstairs for lunch,' Kinza said flatly. She was retreating when Kashish called out.

'I was going to book my ticket to Bangalore.'

Kinza paused. 'And did you?'

'I didn't. I'll stay for a few more days,' Kashish said. 'Especially because I'm doing a collab with Sameer and I want to make it happen before I go back home.'

Kinza's nostrils flared and she walked back inside the room.

'Why are you doing this?'

Kashish wanted to snap at her sister and ask her why it was bothering *her* so much. She held her tongue.

'Because I want to,' she said instead.

'Kashish, what you said out there…'

'Is the truth, Api. You are not my mother.' For years, Kashish had held this truth against her sister. Her sister was not her mother, so to expect her to be more involved in her life hadn't been right. Kinza had a life of her own.

Kinza cocked her head. 'Yes, but I'm your older sister and I do have some rights over you,' she announced. This raised Kashish's hackles. 'And I can't stand by and do nothing when you do something wrong.'

'I'm not doing anything wrong! This is just work,' Kashish insisted. A small white lie was all right. 'And you're a fine one to talk.'

'What's that supposed to mean?' Kinza asked, stiffening a little.

'You and Kaif Bhai had a love marriage, didn't you?'

Kinza's face turned pink as she nodded, so Kashish went on.

'And no one is talking marriage here anyway. We're just working together. Why are you blowing this out of proportion?'

Kinza looked away and then finally her gaze reconnected with Kashish's.

'Fine. Okay, maybe you're right,' she admitted. 'It's just that I still think of you as a little girl and sometimes the reality is a slap in my face. And while you're here, I am responsible for you, whether you like it or not.'

Kashish rolled her eyes. 'Api, I'm an adult.'

'Just being eighteen doesn't meant you're old enough to know any better. You don't have the maturity of an adult.'

Kashish stared at her sister. Had she come here to insult her? But she decided not to push the matter further.

'Anyway, what time are we leaving for the wedding?' she asked. Kinza's eyes narrowed at that.

'So you're coming?'

'Of course. I'm not missing the wedding for anything,' Kashish said.

Kinza rolled her eyes. 'You're going there to meet Sameer, right?'

'For work, yes,' Kashish admitted.

'Hmpf.'

'Whatever.'

'Come down and have lunch.'

'Ya, okay.'

'We're leaving for the wedding at 7 p.m.'

'I'll be ready.'

'I bet you'll be.'

'Api!'

'What?' Kinza turned around at the door.

'Are we good?' Kashish didn't know why she asked her sister that question. It was something that spilled out of her before she could stop herself.

'You tell me, Munni,' Kinza said, and left.

32

Kashish was aware of more than a few women staring at her that evening at the nikah. She'd taken extra care to dress up, which was par for the course, but also because she wanted to make sure that if she bumped into Sameer, he would forget the way she looked this morning, bedraggled and wet, and then in his mom's borrowed clothes.

'That's Misba Apa,' Kinza whispered in her ear as they sat down on the plush chairs. The wedding was being held in an upscale hotel where one floor was allocated for men, and another for women.

Kashish nodded, not sure how she was supposed to behave. Kinza whispered again, and her breath tickled her ear. 'Don't bring up the clothes and all that *here*, okay?'

Kashish nodded. She would have thanked her for the use of her clothes, which would be some sort of awful social faux pas, and she'd never know. But did she really care? It wasn't like she would meet any of these people here again. But it mattered to Kinza, and who knew? Maybe she would meet Sameer's mother again.

Her face turned pink as she wondered at the possibilities. Kinza saw the blush and rolled her eyes.

'Khuda ya…' she muttered.

'I don't remember making fun of you with Kaif Bhai,' Kashish retorted. She put her hand out quickly. 'It's not the same thing. I know. I know. But you're being unnecessarily mean to me.'

Kinza looked startled and then a little shamefaced. She sighed. 'Like I said, it's hard for me to think of you as a grown up.'

Kashish didn't say anything, but her eyes travelled to the two doorways, hoping she would spot Sameer somewhere. But he was obviously on the men's floor and there wouldn't be any chances of him coming here.

This sucked.

She contemplated sending him a message but what would she tell him? Already, she'd put herself in a tough spot by asking him to meet her at the beach this morning.

She opened Instagram and navigated to his profile—she was still not following him. He had posted some new stories. She tapped on one. It had been taken just a few moments ago. Obviously, Sadeem had recorded him, glaring and looking generally annoyed. Sameer kept asking for his phone back but Sadeem who was off camera kept saying 'shut up'.

Pursing her lips, she put her index finger on the screen when Sameer could be clearly seen. The video paused. Her heart skipped a beat. At least it felt like that. He looked so formal and exceedingly handsome.

'A-ha!'

Kashish was so startled, the phone slipped from her hand and fell face down on the carpeted floor.

She looked up to see who it was. Fiza stood by her side, grinning, her hands on her hips. She was wearing a grey and silver sharara that made her look lovelier than the previous night, more so because the grey matched the colour of her eyes. She looked like a fashion model.

Kashish bent sideways to pick up the phone, and smiled at Fiza, hoping she wouldn't give her grief because she'd spotted her on the phone, stalking her cousin's Insta.

'I caught you red-handed!' Fiza said in a singsong voice.

'Shush, please,' Kashish said, looking around. Sameer's mother was thankfully nowhere close.

'If you want to talk to Sameer, you know you can just call him, right?' Fiza said, giving an exaggerated wink that looked hilarious. Kashish bit down on her lower lip to stop herself from laughing.

She wanted to tell Fiza she'd spent the morning with his family, with her Ammajan who kept interrupting the discussions with effusive praise of Fiza, much to Sadeem's disgust. But she didn't say anything.

'I'll call him one of these days. We anyway have to discuss the collab. I'll be leaving for Bangalore soon,' she added in a bid to look cool and anxiety-free.

'I see. So call him then,' she said.

'I will. But not with an audience,' Kashish said, smiling sweetly.

'Are you sure about that?' Fiza asked, glancing at Kashish's phone in her lap.

Kashish looked down and her heart skipped several beats, taking her right to the edge of hyperventilation.

Holy shit. When her phone had fallen down and she picked it up, she'd accidentally tapped the Live button. She was Live, being broadcast to at least ten thousand people who were going berserk, trying to get her attention by leaving comments.

She hunted for the End Live button frantically and quickly tapped on it.

Your Live has ended. 13450 people watched your Live.

She stared at the message on her screen, dumbfounded. She hardly ever did Lives because she liked to keep her audience waiting. It was a treat that she gave them only when she chose to do so. The few times she'd gone Live, she'd had more than fifty thousand people join in to hear her talk.

About nothing.

It was humbling, humiliating and terrifying. At least with the reels, they were scripted beforehand. She always knew what she would do or say. In the Live, she was never really sure of which persona to show the world, and whether they would like it or hate it.

Now, she'd gone and done a Live that may have lasted all of two minutes, proclaiming to the world about her plans for the collab.

Instagram asked her if she wanted to save the video or discard it.

Discard it! She quickly hit the delete button and breathed a sigh of relief.

Fiza was looking at her quizzically. 'What just happened?'

'Well, you startled me into dropping my phone and we went Live,' Kashish was not sure why she wasn't angrier with Fiza. But she couldn't seem to summon any irritation. There was just relief.

'Oh!' Fiza said. 'I'm so sorry.' To her surprise, she sat down on the empty chair beside her and turned to her, brimming with glee. 'I'm so excited about the collab. Not a *single* person in my class will believe that *my* cousin did a collab with you.'

Kashish again wondered how close she was to Sameer.

'Do you have any ideas?' she asked, glancing once at her phone screen and wincing when she saw that her DMs had multiplied dramatically after the aborted Live.

'Oh, I have *plenty*!' Fiza said, crossing her legs daintily and flashing a smile at her as if she had been waiting for Kashish to ask her. Kashish didn't really want to know but asked out of politeness.

'Well…' she prompted.

Fiza sat straighter. 'Okay, here's one. You and Sameer get into a fight about Bangalore and Chennai,' she said.

'Ouch.'

'*Exactly!*' Fiza said, looking excited. 'The two of you can go on and on and then he says…'

'…that you have the beach,' Kashish ended grimly.

Fiza nodded with a clap.

'We do have our Bangalore weather, you know?' Kashish reminded her.

Fiza checked her nails almost absently. 'From what I hear, global warming is making Bangalore *as* hot as Chennai.'

Shit. She was right again. Kashish wanted to tell her about how she'd met Sameer this morning, when they were interrupted.

'Kashish! So lovely to see you again!'

Kashish looked up, startled to see Ammajan walk up to her and open up her arms, as if getting ready to hug her.

Fiza looked at Ammajan and then at Kashish. 'You two know each other?' she asked, her brow furrowing probably trying to recall if she'd introduced them to each other the previous night.

'Of course! Kashish came home with Sameer today.'

Ammajan sat down on the other empty seat, and Kashish looked up just in time to see Fiza's wide eyes. Her face broke into a grin suddenly, and then she gave Kashish a very obvious wink. Kashish was relieved as well as embarrassed. But then her eyes met Kinza's across the room, and her sister didn't look pleased at all.

33

One floor below, Sameer was frowning at his phone. What the hell had just happened? He had been bored. There was hardly a chance he'd meet Kashish so he had surreptitiously started scrolling on Insta, all the while hoping Abbu wouldn't catch him in the act.

Abbu didn't like it when they took out their phones during meal times or most other times. It annoyed him when he saw that now, not just the phone but a ring light stand occupied pride of place in the kitchen because Sameer was shooting his videos there. Just this morning he'd given Sameer a lecture about nothing in particular. How was Abbu so out of touch with reality?

But thankfully, Abbu wasn't around. He was talking to someone, probably discussing politics and the economy. So Sameer looked down at his phone, and was surprised to see that Kashish had gone Live on Instagram.

Shit. Had she accidentally gone Live from here, the wedding? He could see her, but the angle was weird. What was going on? And then, he heard his name.

'If you want to talk to Sameer, you know you can just call him, right?'

His mouth dropped open. He wished he could hear her better. But she realised that the Live had started and shut it down.

Sameer was stumped. It made no sense. Why had he heard his name? *Had* he heard his name? Or was he hallucinating? Had Kashish been flustered?

He had to find out. Time to do what no self-respecting Gen Z-er would do.

He called Kashish.

She cut the call immediately. Rattled, he looked around, hoping no one had seen him make this big blunder. But it was okay, right? It was okay.

To make things worse, he could not stop himself from sending her a text message.

Hey, all good?

Of course it's all good. He rued the moment he hit send and saw the ticks turn blue. What was he doing? Why was he behaving like a complete ass?

Sadeem sat down beside him and exhaled. 'I went to check out the dining area and they haven't started the service yet,' he said, patting his tummy.

'Shush. Don't act like you're a bhukkad who comes to weddings only for the biryani,' Sameer hissed.

'As if you're any better. And what were you doing anyway?'

Sameer needed to tell someone about the Live and how he'd heard his name on it. He also ended up telling

Sadeem that he had called her right after that and sent her a message when she cut the call.

Sadeem's mouth dropped open. 'You are such an idiot. You don't know how to play it cool, do you?'

'Oh, and you know, is it?' Sameer asked, annoyed at his brother's high-handedness.

'Of course,' Sadeem hissed. 'First of all, do not bring up the Live when you talk to her, okay?'

Sameer scratched the back of his neck irritably. 'But…'

'No buts. No talking about the Live. No calling her out of the blue for the love of God. And no talking about the collab either. I'll set it up with Jess.'

Sameer's eyebrows shot up. 'Jess?'

Sadeem gave him an all-knowing smile. 'Yes, Jess. Jessie. I called her earlier. We spoke and came up with a few ideas about the collab. We'll be shooting a couple of reels for us and a couple for her. So we can stagger them and post them later and…'

Sameer put a hand on his brother's elbow, confused. 'When did this happen? Where was I? Shouldn't Kashish and I be involved in all these plans?'

Sadeem nodded. 'Yes, we plan to do a group video call tomorrow morning. Kashish won't be in Chennai for too long so we have to decide fast and shoot quickly. Two kitchen videos for us, one video of the two of you in a café where you can be an annoying person she comes across, and one of her as Aunty K.'

Sameer's head was spinning. 'Whoa.'

Sadeem nodded again. 'You were having your beauty sleep this afternoon when I set up all this with Jess. And by the way, do you know *how much* Kashish pays her?'

Sameer got up, shaking his head. Sadeem followed him as he made his way towards the restroom. He wanted to splash some water on his face.

'Does Kashish know?' he asked finally.

'She...I...um...' For the first time since they started this conversation, Sadeem seemed unsure. 'I don't know. But what's worrying you? It's all good. We're taking care of your stuff, right? You just focus on what needs to be done by you.'

'It's all moving so fast,' Sameer said. He had spent the morning with her in his house and...he looked up startled on hearing his brother laughing.

'How is this moving fast?' Sadeem asked. 'It's a collab. You're not getting engaged to her.'

Sameer's face turned pink but he made a face at his brother and walked into the restroom. He needed some time to think, and some time to decompress. He looked at his phone. Still no reply from Kashish. Here Sadeem was making plans for this collab with Kashish's assistant and she seemed pissed with him for some reason.

What had he done? He'd just called her. Should he try again? Then he thought how his brother would most likely clobber him if he called her again.

But he really wanted to talk to Kashish. He wanted to know what was going on. Could he make an excuse to go upstairs and seek her out? And could he do it without his idiot brother who thought he knew everything, finding out?

34

Kashish tried hard to keep a straight face. Her sister was giving her dirty looks for no reason whatsoever while Fiza listened in shocked silence as Ammajan added way more masala as she recounted Kashish's morning adventure.

'They were both drenched. DRENCHED. You know how much it rained this morning? You would have been tucked into bed because I know you don't wake up for Fajr, lazybones,' Ammajan went on. Fiza opened her mouth to protest but Ammajan steamrolled over her. 'And then this poor girl was shivering. SHIVERING. Sameer came up to me, still in his wet clothes, WET clothes mind you, and tells me that we have to make something that will warm her up. And I thought he was going to make soup. Or ganji. Instead that boy says we'll make SUTRIYAN.'

Kashish had to cover her mouth with her palm. 'Ammajan, you're making it sound way more dramatic than it was.'

'Hush. You listen to my side of the story first,' Ammajan went on.

Fiza leaned closer and whispered, 'Ammajan, keep your voice down. Everyone sitting behind us and in front of us know all the details of this story now.'

Ammajan looked around them with narrowed eyes and both girls started giggling. Whoever was eavesdropping backed off immediately.

'Anyway, where was I? Then he…'

Kashish's phone rang. Startled, she looked down at it and her eyes widened. Sameer was calling her. Without a second thought, she cut the call and turned her phone face down, hoping no one had seen. But of course Fiza had.

She lifted an eyebrow. Kashish blushed. Why had he called her? Unless…oh no…unless he'd seen the Live. Oh no! What were the chances! The timing *was* suspicious and if he had seen the Live, he may even have heard them talk about him.

'Shit,' she muttered under her breath. Fiza was once more absorbed in Ammajan's story but kept glancing her way now and then. Kinza finally managed to free herself and joined them. Kashish immediately stiffened. She didn't want her sister knowing all these unnecessary extra details that Ammajan was adding to the story.

'This is my sister Kinza,' she introduced her to Ammajan and Fiza, who smiled and said salaam.

'I know Misba Apa,' Kinza said with a stiff smile. Ammajan smiled widely.

'Are you from the boy's side or the girl's?' she asked.

While Kinza and Ammajan talked, with Kinza finally warming up to the old lady's charm, Fiza reached out to hold Kashish's hand. 'Come with me to the restroom,' she said.

She and Fiza made their way through hordes of scampering children and gleaming aunties in shiny outfits and jewellery, as everyone waited for the bride to appear.

'Won't you miss the nikah?' Kashish asked.

Fiza shook her head. 'No, not yet. I checked in on Anisa before I came outside to where you guys were sitting. The makeup artist threw a tantrum because no one had told her the *exact* shade of the bride's ghagra and apparently this messed up her palette and she had to fix it.'

'Wow. This sounds like something Aunty K would be interested in,' Kashish spoke without thinking. Fiza clutched her hand excitedly.

'Isn't it? Can we do it *now*? Can we shoot a video in the restroom and you can do an Aunty K spiel?' she asked.

Kashish shook her head. 'No way. A lot goes into making those videos. They need to be planned well ahead of time,' she said. Although that wasn't strictly true. Before Jessie and Rania and Mili had started working with her, it been had just been Kashish with her iPhone. She would make the videos randomly, on her own, with just her ring light and her imagination.

'Oh come on!' Fiza pouted as they pushed open the door to the restroom and walked inside.

'Fiza, I need to work on a script first!' Kashish protested.

Fiza's eyes widened. 'For a thirty-second video?'

Kashish nodded. 'Yes. And sometimes it's longer than that. And it has to hit the mark. I need to have a hook. I can't just do an Aunty K video randomly.'

‘Fine,’ she sighed. ‘Now the real reason I called you here is to ask you what’s going on between you and Sameer?’

Kashish licked her suddenly dry lips. ‘Wow, very direct, aren’t we?’

‘Don’t deflect,’ Fiza meant business.

‘What’s it to you?’ Kashish asked, not sure why she was letting this girl call the shots. She owed her no answers unless she had a personal stake, unless she and Sameer were more than cousins.

‘What does that mean?’ Fiza asked, frowning. ‘He’s my brother. I want to know what’s going on.’

‘So it’s not like your family plans to marry you off to him or something?’ Kashish had to be sure.

Fiza’s eyes widened and she burst out laughing. ‘Ewww…marry *him*? Whatever gave you that idea? Wait, hold that thought. How many Pakistani serials have you watched?’

Kashish looked away guiltily. ‘It’s not like this kind of stuff doesn’t happen here. It’s common enough,’ she said. Why the hell had she brought up *marriage*? What was even wrong with her? It must have been Kinza’s talk about her being of ‘marriageable age’ and all that crap.

Fiza shook her head. ‘No way. I’m not *marrying* Sameer, no matter what. But I take it that you want to be a contender?’

Kashish groaned and slapped her forehead lightly. ‘I don’t want to marry him or anyone right now. I just thought that…maybe there was something between the two of you.’

Fiza made a pukey face. '*Whatever* gave you that idea? And anyway, this isn't about Sameer and me. But Sameer and you.' She gave her a fake sweet smile.

Kashish turned away and tried to gather her thoughts. 'I don't know, okay? Why are you giving me a hard time about this? I don't even know him or you that well for that matter.'

Fiza held her hands up. 'Okay, okay, I get it. Don't get so riled up. But I saw you stalking his Insta account and then moments later, he calls you? And let's not forget this morning when the two of you arrived at his place DRENCHED. How did that happen?' she asked with yet another saucy smile.

Kashish chewed at her lips, then stopped. It would ruin the lipstick. If she told Fiza that she had invited Sameer to the beach, then god only knew what she'd make of it. Everyone was making such a big deal about all of this. Urrgh.

Thankfully right then Fiza's phone rang.

'Oh look who's calling me?' Fiza said, waving her phone in Kashish's face.

'You have his name saved as Snotty Sameer?' Kashish asked with a grin. Fiza's smile vanished.

'Oh shit, he'll *kill* me. But let's see why he's calling,' she said and hit the answer button.

35

Sameer paced the length of the restroom, glancing at the mirror at his reflection, every now and then. He was acting completely out of character, all for a girl. A girl whom he had a crush on, and maybe it was something more too. But what was he going to do about it? And more importantly, what would he do if she didn't feel the same way?

He was going to fixate about all of that later, he decided. What he needed to do now was to think about this collaboration. Sadeem seemed to have taken his duties as his assistant seriously. He had to keep his head in the game too. The Instagram account had seen a huge spurt of growth ever since he started posting his cooking videos regularly, with Ammajan offering her wisecracks. The audience loved her. He imagined for a moment the sort of comments she would make if Kashish was with them and he groaned mentally; but he also knew that the audience would eat it up.

Yet, he couldn't get over the fact that he had called Kashish and she had cut the call. He wanted to know what was going on. Had she changed her mind about the collaboration? Had she decided he was too much of a small fry for her?

That was when he remembered that he had seen a glimpse of Fiza in the Instagram Live. So he dialled her number and waited. When she didn't answer immediately, his anxiety shot up. When the call finally connected, he sensed she was trying hard not to giggle.

Thankfully, before he could say something stupid, she stopped giggling and said, 'You're on speaker phone and Kashish is with me. We're in the restroom actually.'

Sameer scratched the back of his head in confusion. How was he going to ask Fiza anything if they were together?

'I just...um...hey, so it's nothing but...I...not sure...'

'Oh my god, stop *bumbling* so much,' Fiza snapped. 'Did you see the Live? Why were you stalking her, you psycho?'

He heard a gasp and then Kashish's voice: *You can't call people psycho and all that!*

He smiled. 'Yeah, I saw the Live. I wanted to know what was happening.'

'*Nothing* is happening. Unless you make it happen,' Fiza said.

'Like what?' Sameer asked, confused.

'I'm trying to convince Kashish to shoot an Aunty K video here but she's not listening. Maybe you might be able to convince her.'

He didn't hold any sway over her but he tried in any case. 'Kashish, I thought the wedding would be a perfect venue for you to make reels?'

She sighed loudly. 'I don't want to draw any attention to myself right now,' she said. That was odd. He'd seen her talk to complete strangers for her reels sometimes.

Before he could say anything, she spoke again. 'And Aunty K's videos are often shot at home. I need to get into character. I can't just do it on the fly.'

That made sense. He'd noticed that she looked a little different whenever she posted those reels. He didn't know how she made herself look like an older version of herself. Probably, makeup?

Just then, the door to the restroom opened and Sadeem walked inside. 'Are you taking a piss or taking a shower?' he called out loudly and Sameer groaned.

'I'm on a call!' he mouthed.

Sadeem hissed through his teeth. 'Kashish?' he mouthed. Sameer shook his head.

'Okay, that makes sense,' Sameer went back to the call. 'Listen Fiza, I think her assistant and mine are working together to make a proper collaboration happen. You should let things be and not force them.'

'Fine,' Fiza sighed. 'Did you call to talk about that?'

'No, actually…' Sameer frowned. Why had he called? He remembered then. 'Why were you guys talking about me on the Insta Live?'

Sadeem slapped his forehead dramatically, and Sameer turned away so he wasn't looking at his idiot brother. To his annoyance, Sadeem danced his way in front of him, and no matter where he turned, Sadeem was there, mouthing 'play it cool', 'play it cool'.

Fiza spoke. 'I think it's best the two of you talk about this, face to face. Tomorrow, when she comes to your home to shoot a video with you.'

Fiza spoke in tiny pauses, as if she was gauging whatever Kashish was telling her. And then, she hung up.

Sameer stared at his phone while Sadeem grabbed it. 'You are such an idiot. I'm not giving you your phone now. Not until I've set things up with Jessie!' And before Sameer could protest or yank his hair, Sadeem strode out of the restroom.

So help him god, he might just end up going to jail for fratricide if his brother thought he was going to be without his phone until then.

36

Kashish found herself staring at Sameer and Sadeem at her sister's doorstep the next morning. She looked at them in confusion.

'Did I miss some update?' she asked, surprised.

Sadeem shifted on his feet while Sameer gazed back at her and she found that she couldn't meet his eyes.

'Who's at the door, Munni?' Kinza called out.

Groaning mentally, Kashish pulled the door wide open and invited the two of them inside.

'Jess and I got talking,' Sadeem started. 'And we wondered if we could maybe shoot the Aunty K video here today?'

Kashish felt her stomach twist. No! No way! She couldn't do that here. Why hadn't Jess informed *her*? She had to tell them that it wasn't possible. Especially not now.

It was a Sunday morning and the kids were at home. After the excessive kheer and ice cream they'd had the previous night at the wedding, they were still working off their sugar high.

It was chaotic to say the least and Kashish was not amused that she suddenly had to host these two idiots.

Kinza looked at her suspiciously when she led the two boys into the living room.

'What's going on?' she asked, when Kashish left the boys with Kaif Bhai, and she saw them squirm uncomfortably. Served them right for turning up without a word. Thank god she'd woken up and showered already. She was also annoyed at Sameer for not sending a single message after the call last night with Fiza. What was with that? Had she imagined that spark between them? Had she made it all up in her head? Even if nothing else, he could have discussed the videos they were going to shoot.

'I told you, right? Sameer and I are doing a collab together. We're making a few videos that we'll post on both our pages. I'll be doing one in his house where his Ammajan will teach me to cook but he'll also be there.'

Kinza's eyes widened. 'When did you decide all this?' she asked.

Kashish shrugged. 'It just happened, Api. Please don't go making this into a big deal.' She was simultaneously racking her brain on how to spin this situation. Could they shoot the cooking video today instead?

'So you're going to shoot something here? Now?' Kinza asked, excitement lighting up in her eyes.

Kashish shook her head. 'No, it's too noisy here.'

Kinza's face fell. 'I can get the kids to be quiet,' she said after a second.

Kashish winced. 'Yes, but I don't think I can get into the skin of my character right now,' she said, licking her lips nervously.

'Why not?' Kinza asked.

'Kinza! Are you making tea for us?' Kaif Bhai called out.

'No, you come and make it yourself,' she called back and Kashish giggled.

'What?' Kinza asked.

'Nothing. I was just surprised. Shocked actually,' Kashish admitted.

Kinza rolled her eyes. 'You've been here for nearly a week now. Who do you think makes the tea in the mornings?'

Kashish's mouth dropped open.

'But…'

'His tea is better than mine,' Kinza said just as Kaif Bhai walked into the kitchen.

'You needn't have shouted that out,' he muttered as he took out a vessel to make the tea.

'Come, let's go and talk to them and see what plans they have and why you can't shoot your video today,' Kinza said as Kaif Bhai went about making tea. Kashish was mildly impressed. She thought her sister was one of those happy victims of patriarchy who refused to see the truth. Asking her husband to make tea wasn't such a big deal, but it kind of was, in some ways.

Outside, Sameer and Sadeem looked rather stricken as they sat stiffly on the sofa.

'So, Kashish says you can't shoot the video here today?' Kinza jumped into the conversation and Kashish mentally groaned.

Kashish didn't look at Sameer. She was still annoyed with him for springing this on her.

'Why? Why can't you shoot today?' Sadeem asked.

'Well, we need to first finalise a script,' Kashish said, aware of how important that sounded.

'For a thirty-second video?' Sadeem asked disbelievingly.

'Remind me again whose videos have millions of views?' Kashish asked him in a mock sweet voice.

Sadeem sat back, chastised. 'So, you need to work on the script. You and Sameer can do it now and then we'll shoot,' he said.

Kashish shook her head. 'I don't think it's going to work out. Let's shoot the cooking video in your house,' she said.

Sadeem's eyebrows drew together. She was still not looking at Sameer.

Sameer finally spoke up. 'Is there any reason why you don't want to shoot the Aunty K video?' he asked and she stifled a groan. 'I mean those are your most popular videos.'

She swallowed and tried her best not to look at Kinza.

'We could do one in your house or we could do one in a café,' she said stiffly.

'Kashish, I know you're a bigger Instagram star than us. I mean, Sameer,' Sadeem corrected quickly. 'But please can you give it another thought? We'd really like to do an Aunty K video with you.'

She felt trapped. These idiots were going to get her into trouble. 'Let's discuss all this in your house?' she said, getting up.

'What about the tea that Kaif is making?' Kinza spoke up. Kashish turned to her and saw that her sister was looking at her strangely. Shit.

Sadeem and Sameer both looked disappointed but they got up.

'No, no. You boys aren't going anywhere. Sit down and have tea first. And tell me all about this Aunty K,' Kinza said as she settled deeper into the sofa.

37

Sameer felt like he was wading into something unidentifiable. He and Sadeem sat back down reluctantly after being admonished by Kinza. He looked at Kashish for some cues but her face was blank. Almost too blank. Except for her eyes.

Her eyes looked panicked.

Had he done something to make her mad? But how? He hadn't even texted her since Sadeem had his phone until two minutes before they reached here.

It had been a chaotic morning and Sadeem refused to listen to him when he said that they should call Kashish and talk to her first before going to her house straight away. Why ambush her? It was all Sadeem's fault. He said that if they landed up at her place, she wouldn't be able to say no. It was also his fault for giving in to an idiotic seventeen year old. Now, she was staring daggers at them, alternating with pretending that he didn't exist.

While Kinza's husband brought out tea for them, Sadeem was telling Kinza all about Kashish's Aunty K videos. Sameer wondered how come her own sister didn't know about them? True, he had discovered Kashish himself only recently, after she'd chosen to make fun of him, but her videos had been gaining traction over the past couple of years.

Kashish sat stiffly, not moving a muscle. Sameer's mind raced ahead of him. She wanted to do a video with Ammajan at home? Did those videos also need to be scripted?

He noticed that Kashish jerked a little, as if someone had pinched her, while he'd been lost in his own thoughts. Her face paled when Sadeem pulled out his phone and opened Instagram.

'It's best to show them to you, Apa,' he said to Kinza with an ingratiating smile. Kinza smiled back at him, as if he were a cute toddler and not an irritating teenager.

'We're wasting time,' Kashish spoke up.

'Hardly,' Kinza replied as she took the phone from Sadeem's hand. 'This one?' she asked him.

'Yes, they're so wicked and funny and just…' Sadeem was excited, and he seemed to have lost control of his speech because he was making gestures with his hand. Kinza giggled as she played the video.

Sameer watched Kashish close her eyes, as though in defeat. What the hell was going on? Was this a disaster unfolding before him and should he have done something more to stop it?

'This one's really funny,' Sadeem said, leaning across and tapping play on another Aunty K video.

Kinza was smiling and laughing, but as she watched more of the videos, her smile dropped away. Her lips parted as Aunty K defended being a stay-at-home-mother with silly reasons. Sameer had found it funny when he first saw it; now, sitting here, he thought it was a bit insensitive when he looked at Kinza's face.

There was a look of baffled hurt on her face. She didn't look at anyone, not Kashish and not her husband who had finished drinking the tea and was checking something on his phone.

By the time another video ended, the smile had completely disappeared from her face.

'We should go now,' Sameer spoke up. Kashish looked at him, *then*. The look of gratitude on her face wasn't hard to miss.

Kinza didn't protest as the three of them got up. But she looked at Kashish askance. Then she turned to Sameer. 'Where are you guys going?' Before he could answer, she spoke up. 'I know, I know, dinosaurs like me won't know the hip and happening places in Chennai, but I'd like to know where Kashish is going to be.'

The words were delivered in a light tone but there was an undercurrent of something that made him squirm. Sadeem was blissfully unaware of any of this. Kashish looked like she wanted to say something but she kept quiet.

'We're going to our home,' Sadeem said.

Kinza nodded, but didn't say anything. She looked at Kashish and smiled somewhat sardonically. That was when the penny dropped.

Sameer looked between the two sisters. Had Kashish based Aunty K on her own sister? Without asking her permission? Had Kinza discovered it literally just now? That could explain the freezing atmosphere in the living room.

'I'll be back soon,' Kashish said quietly as the three of them stepped out. They'd brought the car and Sameer got behind the wheel. To his surprise, Sadeem sat in the back, leaving the front passenger seat empty.

Kashish slipped into the seat and shut the door.

'Kashish, I really hope you'll do an Aunty K video with Sameer. That's a guaranteed hit,' he said, unaware of the tense atmosphere they'd just left behind.

'Let it go, Sadeem,' Sameer said quietly.

Kashish looked at him, surprised, her face flushed, her eyes wide and alert, and then her face drooped. She almost looked ashamed. Then she sat straighter in the seat and blew out a breath.

'So what are we shooting?'

38

Sameer's home was not as noisy as Kinza's but Kashish still felt a little uncomfortable as they sat at the dining table to discuss the video. Sameer's parents were in the living room and Ammajan was in her bedroom. Kashish wondered just how bad things were going to get once she returned. She may have escaped the immediate fallout, but what would she do if Kinza was going to be mad at her?

She had laughed at the first couple of videos, but it had been a sort of confused laugh, like she wasn't sure it was funny though everyone else seemed to think it was. Then as she'd seen more videos, Kashish knew her sister had finally figured it out.

Should she feel ashamed of herself?

She tried to be defiant, tried to tell herself she'd done nothing that other influencers hadn't done before. So many of them made thinly veiled videos about their mothers and annoying aunts and other such people in their lives. If they could live with it, why couldn't she? She hadn't come outright and said that Aunty K was based on her sister, right?

She glanced at Sameer who had been staring at her and he looked away, his face flushed with embarrassment at having been caught. She felt heat climb over her face slowly. Somehow, Sameer had figured out that Aunty K was based on Kinza. She'd seen the way his expression morphed the moment he understood, and it had pained her.

Why did it matter to her? He was a nobody. But she couldn't negate the burst of feelings inside her any more than she could tell herself she wasn't attracted to him. She had seen it all. His seriousness, his love for cooking, the way, unlike her, he didn't put on a persona for Instagram. What you saw, was what you got.

'What video will we be shooting today, Kashish?' Sameer addressed her, startling her out of her reverie. She turned to look at him. 'Does that need to be scripted as well? Because if you expect me to act, I don't think I can.'

His face was sincere, and there was a sheen of sweat on his forehead. She took in odd details like the tiny nick on his jaw where he'd probably cut himself shaving. And then she looked into his eyes and the world around her receded.

Sadeem cleared his throat and both of them looked at him, startled, as if just remembering he was there.

'I'll go and check why Ammajan is taking so long to get ready,' he said, getting up from the table.

'But…'

'Let him go,' Sameer said, his face serious. 'You never answered my question.'

Kashish pursed her lips as she thought of a suitable reply. Was this a roundabout way of talking about Aunty K? There was a lot of acting involved in the Aunty K videos. Until she'd done the first one, she hadn't thought she had it in her to do it.

'You guys caught me off guard,' she admitted finally. To her surprise, the tips of his ears turned pink as he blushed.

'I would have called you and told you but Sadeem had taken my phone,' he explained.

She cocked her head, disbelievingly.

'Really,' he insisted. His blush deepened. 'He thought I was being unprofessional because I called you and sent you a text last night.'

'So?' she asked, puzzled.

'So he took away my phone, saying I wasn't to be trusted with it.'

Her mouth dropped open. 'And you *let* him?'

He shook his head. 'He was just so stubborn and no amount of arm twisting would make him return my phone to me.'

'I find that hard to believe,' she said with a sudden grin that seemed to startle him.

'Believe me,' he insisted with that same sincerity that made her heart melt. 'I even sat on him last night.'

'You what?' she asked, and it was his turn to grin.

'I sat on him. Tried to squash him. But he wouldn't relent.'

She turned to look at Sadeem. 'What's it like? Having a sibling?'

Sameer stared at her for a long moment, and she realised how it sounded. She shook her head. 'That came out wrong. I meant what's it like to have a sibling your age?'

'It's the worst,' Sameer said easily. 'But it's like living with a friend. An annoying, high-key friend.'

Kashish knew she had to address the elephant in the room. But why? Why should she disturb this equilibrium?

'Let's come up with a couple of scenarios that we can shoot in your house with Ammajan. Let's make it like a tiny skit. Something funny,' she said, changing the subject deftly.

Sameer blinked a couple of times but he nodded. 'Like what?'

Kashish thought quickly. 'So the two of us are arguing about what food to order for dinner and you decide that you can make it better at home?'

He hated the idea, she thought, disappointed. But it was the best she could come up with on such short notice.

'I think it's a bit on the nose, no?' he said finally.

She shut her eyes briefly. 'There's no point being subtle on social media, Sameer,' she said, wishing she didn't sound so school teacherish. 'You did a simple video on kneading atta. I exaggerated it and reshot it. Which video do you think has more views?' Did she sound like a dick? But it was the truth.

'Okay, okay fine. Let's do it. And then what? How does it end?'

'With you being the world's most annoying boyfriend and insisting that we head into the kitchen to cook.' The words just came out, and then they were out there between them.

World's most annoying boyfriend.

Boyfriend.

Uh oh.

'We can have Ammajan give her inputs after that,' she added lamely.

To his credit, Sameer didn't tease her, probably because he was incapable of teasing someone?

'Sure,' he agreed.

39

World's most annoying boyfriend?

The words kept playing back in his head, as the three of them settled down at the table and discussed how to shoot the video. Sameer was flummoxed by how much thought went into it, and he watched as Sadeem and Kashish discussed angles and backgrounds, wishing he had something more to contribute.

When he and Sadeem shot the cooking videos, they just set up the ring light stand in the kitchen and shot the videos which Sadeem edited later and uploaded on his account. He'd never realised that Kashish's videos looked so much better because of the planning that went into making them.

At the same time, he was also aware of something unsightly having unfolded back in her sister's home and Kashish was delaying her return. He wondered how long Kashish could stay out and not face the music.

Ammi ventured into the dining room, smiling at Kashish and asking if they wanted to have lunch before or after the shoot. Kashish looked a little uncomfortable but she thanked her for lending her clothes to her. Ammi brushed it off. Sameer knew he would have to face her inquisition later on. Sadeem suggested they eat afterwards and he agreed. Right now, he couldn't face the prospect of eating anything.

Ammajan emerged from her room and all of them stared.

'What?' she asked, looking down at her neon pink saree.

Sameer exchanged a look with Kashish who kept a straight face.

'Are you guys making some sort of mithai for the video?' Ammi asked, not moving her gaze from Ammajan.

'Why?' Ammajan asked.

'Because you're wearing mithai pink?' Ammi laughed.

Ammajan shook her head and shimmied her shoulders, looking a bit like a Bharatnatyam dancer. 'Ahahahah,' she said. 'I'm the one who will be in Kashish's video. I have to look good, no?'

Ammi rolled her eyes and Ammajan felt compelled to explain further. 'Her videos get millions of views,' she said in a hushed, conspiratorial voice. Ammi looked duly impressed but Sameer could sense that Kashish was embarrassed.

'So what are we making today?' she asked him, as Sadeem brought the ring light stand from the kitchen.

When he was not being distracted by Kashish's presence in his home, Sameer was trying hard to think of what they would make today. He usually made south Indian style Muslim food on his account—kali mirch ki phaal, khatta baingan, daalcha, to name a few. He'd planned to shoot a video of him making biryani when they'd reached some sort of milestone. He also interspersed these videos with him making some sort of trending food, like the time he'd made churros or cloud bread or baked gulab jamun as these got him a lot of views and likes and more followers.

'A snack?' Sadeem suggested. Cooking something complicated would take a lot of time.

'But we're doing that skit, remember?' Kashish said. 'So it would have to be something you'd have for dinner.'

In the end, they decided on a simple white sauce pasta. Ammajan was not impressed. Whenever Sameer made something that was not traditional, Ammajan's commentary became funnier.

It took them a while to set up everything, from the skit, to their entry into the kitchen. Abbu came over to watch, and his expressions were a thing to behold. Sameer was awful at the acting bit. He had told Kashish he couldn't act but she had waved it off, saying it was okay. Now she was regretting her decision, he thought. What was worse was having his parents watching them as they discussed what to order for dinner.

Kashish sensed his discomfort and looked up at everyone. 'Sadeem, can you set up everything in the kitchen? And Ammajan, if you can just make sure he does it properly?' she suggested. Then she smiled and quietly asked his parents to leave. Ammi threw him a narrow-eyed look but nodded and walked away. It was just them now. Kashish made adjustments to the phone and walked back to sit next to him at the dining table.

'Just relax,' she said with a smile.

With her sitting so close to him, it was going to be impossible, he decided, feeling even more un-relaxed. The truth was, Sameer had never felt this alive. Pleasure skirted just below the surface of his skin and he wasn't sure how to classify it. Was it because of a Sunday well spent with someone like Kashish? Was it because of the 'boyfriend' comment?

He desperately wanted to ask her what she meant by the boyfriend remark but he didn't want to sound foolish.

He didn't even know when she had started acting, because it seemed natural and real as she asked him what they were having for dinner. He tried not to think of the phone or his family floating around the house as he answered her.

Then they did it again. And again. Until she was satisfied that he was conversing with her and not acting. Finally, she sighed and nodded.

'That should do,' she said.

'How do you do this all the time?' he asked, already exhausted.

She smiled, and some of the exhaustion leaked away. 'I've got a team who helps me but I've gotten used to it,' she said. Then she held his hand and stood up, so he got to his feet as well.

'We have to shoot the kitchen section now,' she reminded him.

'Is that going to be scripted too?' he asked.

She shook her head. 'No, you forget I'm here. You cook and I'll talk to Ammajan,' she said.

How was he going to forget that she was there? It was impossible.

But between them, they actually managed to shoot the video using three phones—his, hers, and Sadeem's. Ammajan's commentary in Dakhni Urdu cracked Kashish up and the lightness in her eyes made him feel like he could do anything he put his mind to as well.

'I'll edit it and post it, adding you as a collaborator,' she said when they were finally finished.

It was a late lunch for them, but no one seemed to mind and he was grateful about that. Abba could have easily said something annoying but for some reason, he didn't say anything but just observed how Sadeem and Kashish had paired up to tease Ammajan about something.

'Nalayakh bacche!' Ammajan said with fond exasperation, reaching over to lightly twist Sadeem's ears.

When lunch was over and everyone had dispersed, the three of them continued to sit at the dining table and look at the videos.

'I don't know about you two, but I think I deserve an afternoon nap after that lunch,' Sadeem yawned and with a wave at Kashish, he walked away, leaving the two of them ostensibly alone.

Kashish too seemed to realise it as she collected her things. She was the bigger Instagram star, but the video they had shot together was quite adorable. He couldn't wait to see it go up. He couldn't wait to see how she'd edit them together. A tiny part wondered if he was setting himself up for disappointment. What if she decided to edit it in a way that showed him in an unflattering light?

But she wouldn't do that. Not when she had worked equally hard at getting everything right. Would she? How well did he even know her to make any sort of assumptions about her?

So, he ended up asking her something else altogether. One that he normally would never have asked, because it was intrusive and personal. But sometime during this weird day, the normal walls had collapsed and Sameer just plunged in.

'Is everything going to be okay at home?' he asked. Her head shot up immediately but she didn't say anything right away. Neither did she cut him down for being cheeky or intrusive.

She sighed softly. 'It's complicated.'

'I have time.'

She looked annoyed for a second before the expression morphed into one of resignation. 'I don't know how to say this without sounding like a horrible person.'

He processed that in silence for a few seconds. 'Well, if you acknowledge that, then you've taken the first step already.'

'First step towards what?' she looked puzzled.

'Towards forgiveness. Redemption,' he suggested, feeling like a huge pit had opened up in his stomach at the way her expression tightened. But he wasn't going to back down even as her eyebrows arched.

'Forgiveness? I'm not apologising to anyone,' she said.

'But you just said you…that thing about being a horrible person.'

'I grew up thinking I had two mothers,' she began.

Sameer hadn't expected this. He sat still, not sure how to respond to her statement.

'Kinza Api is sixteen years older than me. I don't know what my parents were thinking when they had such a huge gap between their kids...I don't think they were thinking at all.' She blushed and shuddered at the same time. 'Anyway, as I grew up, I used to think of my mother as badi Ammi and Kinza as chhoti Ammi. I never voiced it though, because I knew people would think I was being cheesy or adorable. But we were never siblings like others. Like the two of you.'

Sameer nodded, glad that Sadeem had left.

'So when Kinza Api got married and left, it broke my heart. But I was okay with it. After a little while, I figured that of course she'd get married and leave. It was just my parents and I but she visited every now and then. It wasn't the same, but I got used to it eventually. Then my mother died.'

Sameer didn't stop to think. He reached out and covered Kashish's hand with his own. She looked up at him with suspiciously shiny eyes but didn't pull her hand back.

'She came over and stayed with us for long periods of time,' Kashish explained. 'I don't know why I assumed she'd leave Kaif Bhai and stay with us forever. But in my head, it was like, now that Ammi is gone, Api would have to take her place, right? God, I know how messed up that sounds, but I was just thinking of her as someone who would take my mother's place. Or at least, make my mother's loss hurt less.'

Sameer watched her face intently, aware of the privilege he was being afforded of this glimpse into her inner world.

He didn't know what he'd done to earn it but he would try his best not to be unworthy of it.

'And then, one day she tells us that they're moving away to Chennai. That Kaif Bhai wants to live closer to his parents.'

It was like the hurt was still fresh for her. She still looked like a baffled ten year old. 'I couldn't understand it. She couldn't just leave me and go. But there she was. Going away, leading her life.'

Sameer still didn't understand how this tied into the Aunty K videos but he bided his time silently, pressing his thumb into the soft skin of her palm. Her eyes flared and she took a deep breath and pulled away her hand from his.

'I realised only now that I was being unfair to her. She couldn't take my mother's place because she wasn't my mother. But try telling that to ten-year-old me? My resentment with her grew and grew, especially when she had her own babies. I felt like I had stopped being the most important person in her life. I knew I wasn't, even then, but with the kids, she changed even more.'

Kashish looked troubled and Sameer realised belatedly that she was working all of this out in her head at this very moment, and he was entirely extraneous. She seemed to have even forgotten that he was sitting here. She was coming to terms with her own feelings and her reactions.

'She became more and more like Ammi. And it hurt that all that tenderness was now directed towards someone else. I know it's selfish of me, but it is what it is. I felt angry, cheated, and unnecessary, all at once. Then a couple of years ago, for some reason I was wearing one of her kurtas that she'd left at home. Maybe my laundry wasn't done or I don't know why. But I found myself channelling her. Then, it just kept getting easier. The more I made videos about her imagined life in Chennai, the more I mocked her, the less hurt I felt.'

She stopped speaking and looked up at him, a look of growing horror in her eyes. 'I'm a terrible person, right? I should…I should…'

Overwhelmed, she got up and shook her head.

'I need to leave,' she said and nearly ran from there.

Sameer cursed under his breath and ran out after her, ignoring his puzzled parents in the living room.

40

Kashish couldn't bear the quiet judgment in his eyes. She had to leave. She really didn't want to make a scene, so she didn't run out of there like she wanted to. God, she was making such a big fool of herself. Normally she was so reserved and in control of her emotions. What had gotten into her?

She walked out from there swiftly, not looking at his parents, her heart knocking around in her ribs, feeling like any moment it would jump out. The entire day felt surreal.

Kinza now knew she was the inspiration for Aunty K and there was no way she could spin it to make herself look better. She was guilty of mocking her sister online, in a way that had gotten her lakhs of followers. In fact, so much of her popularity and fame was due to the Aunty K videos although she had started diversifying her content so as to not get bracketed in that avatar.

And now, Sameer knew it too.

No one had asked her about the Aunty K videos, assuming that it was all imaginary and in good fun. In fact, even Rania hadn't deduced it. So it had been disconcerting that someone she didn't know at all had made the connection. What's more, he'd somehow made her talk about all that stuff.

She was a little in shock. What on earth had possessed her to tell him all that?

She walked swiftly, hoping she could just jump into an auto and tell them to take her to Kinza's home, where she was going to…shit…she was going to have to face her sister. Also, she didn't know Tamil and she was sure that the auto drivers would fleece her if she didn't use a ride app.

'Kashish!'

She froze and then sped up her pace. She hadn't expected him to follow her. She felt foolish. What was it about this boy that had prompted her to open up her heart? Why had she told him all those mortifying things about herself?

She wanted to rewind the last half hour. She stopped walking and turned around.

'Hey where are you going?' he asked.

'Home,' she replied and made to turn when he reached out and put his hand on her elbow. The contact burned. His gaze was intent, his eyes moving swiftly over her face, as if trying to read her like a book. Each time his eyes tracked her face, she felt an answering tingle and she didn't know what it meant.

'Look, I'll drop you home,' he said.

She wanted to say no. But he pursed his lips and leaned forward. 'Please? I don't know what happened back there but it felt important and I don't want you to go away when you're upset.'

The tumultuous feelings inside her kept growing.

'Okay,' she said.

He looked relieved and together they walked towards the car. She was glad no one had been around when they'd talked. She quite liked Sadeem, but he was the opposite of Sameer in every way and she wasn't sure she could be around his abrasive and in-your-face behaviour. Not now when she was feeling so vulnerable.

Sameer…he was like a quiet, balmy breeze that didn't ruffle her, but lifted the edges of her consciousness, and gave comfort in a way she hadn't ever expected from anyone else.

Not since Ammi. Not since she realised there wasn't anyone she could turn to, with the complete assurance that the person would get them.

The epiphanies kept coming and she didn't know how much more she could take. In silence, they got inside the car. Warily, she pulled out her phone to see if Kinza had texted her, asking her where she was and why she hadn't come home for lunch.

Nothing.

It felt like a sharp pain behind her sternum. Her sister was rightfully mad at her. She had to figure out a way to fix this. Did that mean she had to apologise? God, she hated apologising. Also, why did she need to apologise? She hadn't publicly outed Aunty K as her sister. So what if she poked fun at everything she represented?

But she knew this was a losing battle. The dread grew inside her at the thought of having to talk to Kinza about all this.

Just tell her what you told Sameer.

Oh god, no. Getting it out just once had been bad enough. Telling it all to Kinza would be so humiliating.

Sadeem glanced at her as he started the car. Heat swirled in her belly. What was she going to tackle first? The mess with Kinza or this growing attraction to Sameer?

Sameer lifted his eyebrows questioningly.

'Can we just go somewhere we won't be disturbed?'

Oh god, no. She hadn't actually said that, had she?

Then she looked at his blushing face as he started the car and mortification stained her cheeks. Her mouth and brain were not in sync apparently because she'd said it out. Aloud.

41

In the end, they settled for driving to the beach but they didn't get out of the car. Sameer wasn't sure what to say and the uncomfortable silence stretched before them. He wasn't sure how this had happened or why, but he was glad that he was spending his Sunday afternoon with Kashish.

Yes, he excused her behaviour mostly because she was pretty and he liked her a lot. Yes, he knew it was shallow of him.

But as he glanced at her staring out of the window at the empty-ish beach, he wondered what was going on in her head. Was she regretting telling him everything?

Some moments later, she turned to him. 'Thank you,' she said softly.

He shrugged. 'For what?'

'For doing this.'

He didn't trust himself to say the right thing at the moment. If she had been in a better mood, he might have joked with her about it, but he didn't think she'd appreciate it now.

'It's okay,' he managed finally.

She tucked her hair behind her ear.

The silence between them stretched. This time she wasn't looking out of the window at the waves crashing on the beach. She was looking at him.

His heart raced. His mouth felt dry. Was he hyperventilating? Was his breath coming faster than it should? But he couldn't look away.

She was the prettiest sight he'd seen in his life. Her eyes were huge and there was a world of worry in them, but she still looked stunning. She surprised him by reaching out and picking up his hand and inspecting it, and then looking back at him.

Go for it.

'I really like you, Kashish.' The words tripped out of his mouth before he could hold them back in and while he was horrified internally, he tried to keep his face impassive. Or broody, which was apparently a thing, according to his brother.

Her lips parted in surprise. They had both unbuckled the seat belts when he had parked the car. But still, seeing her move towards him shocked him.

What is she doing? What is she doing?

The litany erupted in his head as her fingers skated over his jaw and her thumb rubbed at something at the corner of his mouth. His pulse jumped, like he'd been electrified.

But she didn't seem fazed. In fact, the air between them vibrated with tension.

'I like you too,' she whispered.

Instinct spurred him closer. He cupped her face and she moved close enough that he could attempt to count her eyelashes.

It was a soft kiss, at first. Heat and shock swirled in his belly, growing into an inferno when she pulled him towards her. And then, she held his face between her hands and kissed him.

The kiss sent him tumbling over some edge and he tried hard not to fall. He pulled away and stared at her.

What happened next? Where did they go from here? He didn't want to speak and snap the magic of the moment. In fact, he was afraid it would break if he breathed wrong. But they were sitting in a parked car overlooking a public beach. They had to talk…they had to…

'Can you drop me back home?' she asked softly.

Disappointment flooded him, but he knew this wasn't easy for her. Unless it was. Unless she did this all the time.

No. No he wasn't going to go there. It was none of his business, even though he was dying to make it his. What they had between them was tentative and new and he wasn't going to ruin it by coming off as a Neanderthal.

He cleared his throat. 'Sure.'

The silence in the car was thick as he drove away from there. Was it regret? Or was it dismay? Had it been a bad kiss? He had no idea because he'd been too swept up in the moment to think about the mechanics of it. He'd acted on instinct. Maybe he should have…

She surprised him by putting her hand on his elbow. He didn't look at her because they were in the middle of traffic, and his heart warmed when she didn't pull away. At a signal, he finally turned his head, just as she took away her hand.

What did this mean? Why wasn't there a handbook that he could use to decode all these moments? And what happened next? Did he call her? Did he have to wait for a certain period of time? And what about when she returned to Bangalore? Were they a thing now? Was this a long-distance relationship? Was that what she wanted? Was this even a relationship? On the basis of one kiss? One mind-blowing kiss, nevertheless.

She sighed loudly and he glanced at her quickly.

'What?' he asked, glad his voice didn't come out as strangled as it felt.

'I feel like you're overthinking this,' she said quietly.

He looked at her, a little amazed. 'Are you a mind reader?'

She smiled and shook her head. 'I can read your face though.'

He hoped not. God, he really hoped not. He didn't reply, not sure what to say but glad that she had broken the tense silence between them.

'Sameer, can we just take each day as it comes? For now?'

No. He wanted his future mapped out and he wanted to know if she featured in it. But he knew if he said that, this wouldn't move further and everything would grind to a halt.

He wanted to ask, for how long. But he bit down the words, and nodded instead. Then he found himself turning to her, and he couldn't help himself. He picked up her hand and kissed her knuckles briefly. She didn't pull her hand away.

That had to mean something. Right?

42

Kashish didn't know if she had jumped from the frying pan into the fire, but it sure did feel like that. And well, the fire was most delicious.

She had no idea that was going to happen when she told Sameer they should go somewhere they wouldn't be disturbed. Especially, the kiss. Okay, it's not like she hadn't considered it or thought of it, and she'd had a couple of dreams where it had already happened, but each time she would snap awake just when the kiss was getting into proper kiss territory.

She didn't look at him again, not because she was embarrassed but because she was sure that if she did, she would ask him to stop the car and kiss her again. And that would be even more embarrassing.

She meant it when she asked him if they could take each day as it came, but a part of her wanted something deeper, a more meaningful connection that defied the logistics of how they would manage a long-distance relationship. She could see that her question hadn't pleased him but she needed time to think about this and how quickly it was getting important for her.

They'd both admitted that they liked each other. And she had an inkling now of what Rania meant when she went on about her boyfriend Aamir, and how he made her feel. But Kashish didn't feel anything like *she was going to die without him*. Please. It was nothing dramatic like that, which was nice. She liked Sameer and she enjoyed the kiss. Even though curiosity had spurred her, she felt that underneath it all there was the foundation for something more serious.

Thoughts of the kiss skittered away when they reached Kinza's home. Anxiety roiled inside her once more. Should she just pretend that nothing was wrong? Could she act like she had no idea why Kinza was possibly pissed off with her?

'Just talk to her about it. Tell her what you told me and she'll understand,' Sameer said, startling her out of her thoughts. She looked at him in disbelief. Was he for real? Did he actually think she was going to instigate the conversation about something she'd rather bury deep under the carpet and never look at again?

'Thanks for dropping me,' Kashish said tightly, and he frowned. It made him look irritatingly hotter but she ignored the dip in her belly.

He cleared his throat as she undid her seat belt and she looked at him.

'I still think we should do an Aunty K video together,' he said quietly.

'Yes, I'll get Jessie to fix up the date with Sadeem,' she said. He looked at her face, almost incredulously now. What? Just because they'd kissed didn't mean that the rules of engagement about this collaboration had changed. Right? Yes, so they liked each other and she had inadvertently given him insights into how her mind worked. But that didn't mean anything else had to change.

She got down from the car and pushed the gate open and walked up the steps. At the door, she turned to see if he was still there.

He was. But he wasn't looking at her. He was looking straight ahead. Fine. Sulk if you want, she thought, annoyed. She didn't bother waving at him because he wouldn't see it anyway. She rang the doorbell and waited. As the door opened, she heard the sound of the car starting.

Some small part of her was annoyed with herself too. She needn't have been so…so…cut and dried? Practical? But this was how she was. She couldn't and she wouldn't change herself for anyone. Certainly not for a guy.

She was expecting Kinza at the door but instead, it was Kaif Bhai who opened and he smiled at her absently as he ushered her inside.

'Where's Api?' she asked. She needed to know what her mood was like, so she could gauge how much to avoid her.

'She's taking a nap.'

Okay, so that gave her a little breathing room. But for how long? Well, as long as it would take to pretend that nothing had happened. If they didn't talk about it, then it hadn't really happened, right?

There was no way she could tell her sister all that she had told Sameer. That had been a lapse of judgment probably brought on by her attraction towards him. Although, to be fair, that didn't seem very logical. The things she'd told him should have made him want to run away in the opposite direction.

Instead, he'd kissed her.

Her cheeks flamed and she walked up the stairs to her room, surprised that the house was so quiet on a Sunday. She hadn't seen the kids downstairs, so maybe they were napping with Api in her room.

Kashish went to her room and shut the door and with her back to it, tried to make sense of all the tumultuous emotions and thoughts that were swirling through her, vying for attention.

Sameer. Kinza. Instagram. The kiss. Videos. The kiss. Kinza. The kiss.

Okay, the kiss had been wonderful. Not sloppy or weird like she'd imagined it would be. It had left her feeling warm and wanted. It had made her feel like she was a part of something, that she mattered to someone outside of familial duty. Yes, Abbu and Kinza loved her, but that was by default. They had to. Sameer's feelings on his transparent face had told her another story altogether.

And she'd crushed it before the spark could grow. Was she always going to sabotage this stuff? She'd liked boys in college before but she'd felt none of the flaming attraction that she'd felt towards Sameer. This entire trip was tinged with something special because of him.

She was such a fool. She had to apologise to him and hoped he would understand why she constantly teetered between extremes. She hoped he wouldn't give up on them already.

The situation with Kinza was not going to explode this very moment, so she could text him, she decided. But then he'd be driving. And she didn't want him to check his phone while he drove.

She mulled over his words, his soft encouragement about talking over things with Kinza, and despite her attraction and feelings, she felt that tiny burst of irritation erupt once more. He couldn't assume that just talking over things was the solution. He didn't know her. He didn't know their family. Yes, she had given him a rundown of what had happened, but that didn't make it okay for him to make assumptions about how other families worked.

She thought of his family, and knew that things were probably very different there. There was an easy camaraderie and an exasperated sort of affection that they all held towards each other. She'd especially enjoyed spending time with Ammajan. In her own house, everything had fallen apart once Ammi died.

She didn't know how long she sat there, when there was a knock on the door. Startled, she opened the door to find Kinza at the threshold.

'We need to talk,' she said.

Why? What's the need? Who cares? What's going to change?

But Kashish pulled the door open wider and Kinza walked inside.

43

Kinza walked up to the bed and sat down at the edge. She looked tired and her eyes were red-rimmed. All of a sudden, Kashish was anxious. She wanted this to be over quickly and for them to be on the other side of it. But she couldn't bring up the topic. She couldn't make herself say the words. So she sat in this uncomfortable silence until her sister spoke.

Kinza cleared her throat.

Kashish winced but she licked her dry lips.

'I've been thinking,' Kinza began.

Kashish looked straight ahead. She wasn't going to help her sister out by prompting her or pre-empting her words.

'I think it's time Abbu got married.'

There was a high-pitched buzz in her ears and Kashish turned to Kinza, not sure if she'd heard right.

'What?' she asked, hoarsely. 'What do you mean?'

Kinza looked defiant. 'I meant what I said. It's time Abbu got married.'

Again, it sounded so absurd that Kashish couldn't understand if they were actual words. 'Why?'

'What do you mean why? He's all alone. Once you get married and move away, he's going to be completely alone.'

Heat buzzed under her skin. Her sister could *not* be serious.

'Did Abbu *say* he wants to get married?'

Get married. Abbu *was* married. To Ammi. How could Kinza say this so casually?

'I've been meaning to talk to him about it. Look, it's been almost ten years since Ammi passed away. And Abbu is all alone. He needs...'

'Someone to cook for him? We have Akka for that,' Kashish snapped.

Kinza gave an exasperated sigh that turned defensive. 'So you're saying that a wife's role is only to cook?' she asked. Her tone was challenging, as if she was expecting Kashish to finally address the elephant in the room that was Aunty K.

'I didn't say that. But...but why does he need to get married? He's perfectly happy right now.'

'Spoken like a child who doesn't want to look at the truth even when it's glaring in her face,' Kinza said, with a huff.

'Child?' Kashish asked, outraged.

'Yes. You are being a child if you can't understand that Abbu is lonely. You're not his companion. You're his daughter and you won't be with him all your life. He needs to live his own life and he's still so young.'

'He's sixty,' Kashish said, nostrils flared.

'Sixty is still young, Kashish,' Kinza's voice was rising.

'And what about Ammi?' Kashish asked, panic growing inside her at the realisation that once more, the adults in her life were going to get their way, make the changes they wanted whether she wanted it or not.

'What about Ammi?' Kinza asked, puzzled.

'She just disappears completely?'

Kinza sighed the sigh of someone trying to explain a difficult concept to a child. 'Kashish, Ammi passed away. Nearly a decade ago.'

'And now you want to obliterate her memory too?' Kashish asked, hysteria building inside her.

Kinza shook her head. 'No one said anything about that. Ammi will always be Ammi. This isn't for us, Kashish. This is for Abbu.'

And what about me? The words were on the tip of her tongue but she was breathing so hard that she couldn't think clearly. Everything was getting jumbled up in her head. This was worse than what she'd imagined Kinza would tell her about Aunty K. This was...this was unacceptable. She wouldn't stand for it. She would run away from home if Abbu got married. This other woman would never be her mother, and she would never, ever call her Ammi.

All of this was visible on her face because Kinza's face softened and she put her hand on her shoulder.

'Munni, listen. We can't be selfish. We're young. We have our lives ahead of us. Abbu doesn't have to spend the rest of his life all alone, pining for Ammi and being without a companion.'

Blood roared in Kashish's ears. 'Would you have done the same for Ammi?' she asked finally.

'What?' Kinza asked, confused.

'If the situation had been reversed, would you have been so sympathetic towards Ammi's loneliness?' her voice now growing into a shout as the answer was clearly written on Kinza's face.

Her sister's expression morphed into one of confusion but also something quite like exasperation and defiance.

'I knew it,' Kashish yelled. 'All this is one-sided. And it's all a pretence.'

'What's a pretence?' Kinza asked, putting her hand on Kashish's wrist. But Kashish yanked it away.

'This pretence that you care about us at all. You don't. You don't care about me, Abbu or Ammi. You just want to feel good about yourself. If you would never have suggested to Ammi that she remarry because she was lonely, then you know you're a hypocrite, right?'

Self-righteous anger was fuelling her tirade, combined with a feeling that she may have been right after all in lampooning her sister. Her sister didn't deserve her apology.

'Kashish, listen, it's not the same thing and…'

'How is it not the same thing?' Kashish stood up. Kinza got up as well.

'You deserve all that I've done in the name of Aunty K,' Kashish blurted out. Kinza's face turned pale and her nostrils flared.

'I was willing to put that behind and be civil with you because this discussion is important,' Kinza shouted back.

'Don't. Don't be civil, Api. Tell it like it is!' Kashish said, her chest heaving. She could feel tears prickling at the corners of her eyelids and her throat felt poky and hot.

'My own sister, my little baby sister thinks she can use me for cheap laughs from people on the internet,' Kinza said in a hushed whisper but Kashish didn't feel bad for even one second.

'Because you deserve it. You're a hypocrite and you know it. You only care for yourself and *your* family. You forgot all about me when you got married and then when you had your insufferable brats, I completely ceased to exist!' Kashish's breath was coming in pants. Was she having a heart attack? A panic attack?

'I'm not going to stand here listening to this bullshit,' Kinza said, walking away from there.

'Go, go away like you always do. I'm anyway an interlude in your life. I'm no one important,' Kashish shouted. She was going to book her tickets for tomorrow morning and go to Bangalore right away. She couldn't stay here for another minute. She was not going to come out of this room at all. She wasn't…

There was the sound of thuds, followed by a muffled scream and then there was silence. Her skin still felt too tight but Kashish had a horrible realisation that something bad had happened. She ran outside just as Kinza rolled down the last step, and landed with a sickening thud, blood seeping from her head.

44

Sameer reached home in a daze. He didn't know what had transpired between him and Kashish because one moment, he'd been holding her hand, day dreaming about the kiss, and the next, she was talking to him like he was a mere acquaintance.

He bristled with indignation that lasted for all of five minutes. How dare she treat him like that? But then as he parked the car in its spot, some of the anger deflated and he was troubled at the direction of his thoughts. When had he become an all or nothing guy? Wasn't Kashish being sensible in telling him they should try and live in the moment and not make any plans?

But making plans was his thing. He made plans constantly. Nothing made him happier than to tick to-do items off his lists. Sometimes, just making a plan was enough. Kashish's life was carefully planned out too, he'd seen that. On Instagram her posts appeared natural and casual but they were carefully curated, and she worked hard on every aspect of those.

So what was this resistance to them being together? God, why was it so hard to understand women? He ground his teeth in frustration as he unlocked the door to the house and walked inside.

Sunday evenings usually had a fixed pattern. Everyone either went out together somewhere, or they stayed at home and watched a movie on Netflix. Today, neither of those options was happening. His parents weren't around and Sadeem was using the opportunity of a free TV to watch a football match.

'Hey! What happened, Romeo? Where did you disappear with Kashish?' he asked him with a wink.

Sameer blushed and felt like an idiot. There was no way he was going to tell anything to his brother. Well, certainly not about the kiss. But he had to talk about everything else that had happened, or he'd go stir crazy.

'Where's Abbu and Ammi?' he asked.

'Ammi managed to rope Abbu in for a bit of shopping and Ammajan went along with them,' Sadeem said.

Sameer's eyebrows went right up into his hairline. 'What? How?'

Sadeem shrugged. 'Beats me. They were leaving just when I woke up from my nap.' Usually Abbu behaved like he was allergic to shopping. Literally.

'So it's just us then?' Sameer settled on the sofa, stretching out his legs.

'Yes, so you can spill. What happened?' Sadeem stretched out the last two words with a sort of anticipation in his voice.

We kissed.

No. NO way.

'We kind of admitted that we liked each other,' Sameer said. That much, he could tell his brother.

'And?' Sadeem asked, eyes wide, football match abandoned.

'And she wants to take each day as it comes,' Sameer said, still puzzled at what it actually meant.

Sadeem sat back, with a disappointed sigh.

'Ah. Then she probably doesn't like you very much and she was letting you down easily,' he said.

Sameer's head swivelled towards his brother. 'What?' he asked, something twisting his gut in a low and dangerous way.

Sadeem shrugged. 'If you told a girl you liked her, I doubt that would have been her response if she really liked you back.'

Sameer was unable to control himself. 'But we kissed,' he blurted out.

Sadeem whooped. 'I knew it! I knew you were holding back something!'

Annoyed that his brother had manipulated him into revealing everything, Sameer jumped on him and tackled him on the ground. Sadeem flailed and tried to get up but his brother's arm was around his neck in a way that would have made Ammi shriek in horror if she'd been around. But Ammi wasn't around and this brat was going to get it.

Sadeem punched his tummy hard and Sameer's grip loosened and soon, he was in Sadeem's chokehold. Flushed, sweaty, both boys wrestled each other aimlessly, almost knocking over the coffee table and making a mess of the living room.

'Enough. Enough,' Sadeem panted as he put up his hand in surrender. 'You have two years on me. I'm still growing.'

Sameer sat up, adjusted his T-shirt and glanced at the destruction they'd caused. 'We'd better clean this up before the parents get back.'

'Why?' Sadeem asked, leaning back against the sofa that had been pushed way behind its usual spot.

'What do you mean why?'

'I mean why can't we just leave it a mess and have them come back and yell at us?' Sadeem asked.

'I don't want them to yell at me.'

'I don't mind. I'd rather listen to Ammi yell at me than clean up. Ouch! Let go!' Sadeem screeched because Sameer had twisted his ear and had pulled him up. 'This is child labour and you know it!'

But the two of them got down to cleaning up everything in companionable silence. 'And then?' Sadeem asked, as he flung himself back on the sofa and picked up the AC remote.

'And then what?'

'What happened after the kiss?'

Sameer was just glad his brother hadn't asked him *about* the kiss itself, so he sighed and told him about their conversation when he dropped her off. Was it foolish to expect any sort of meaningful analysis from a seventeen year old?

Sadeem listened in silence as Sameer told him everything except the Aunty K and Kinza connection, and all that Kashish had told him about herself. That was not his secret to share.

'Well?'

'Okay, maybe she doesn't like it when guys are possessive and I know you like things defined and you like structure, but this doesn't sound so bad, bro. Maybe just take her words at face value and take each day as it comes?'

Sameer scowled. 'And the Aunty K video she's going to shoot with me, she said she'll get it organised between you and Jessie.'

'So?' Sadeem asked.

Sameer opened his mouth to say something but he shut it. Yeah, so? Why was he pissed about that? Their personal equation didn't have to intrude on the professional collaboration. He should be glad she was clear cut about that. But he didn't have to like it. It sucked.

He opened his mouth to say something when his phone rang. His belly reacted most unsuitably when his mind thought that it could be her. But it wasn't. It was Ammi.

He answered the call and immediately, knew something was wrong. Was it Abbu? Was it Ammajan? He'd never heard Ammi speak in such a hushed and stilted voice. Heavy rocks settled into the pit of his stomach.

'Kashish's sister Kinza slipped and fell down the stairs and hurt her head. She's in the hospital. I just got to know,' she said.

Stunned, Sameer stood up. 'Which hospital?' he asked in a choked voice.

'Why?' Ammi sounded surprised. 'She's in the ICU and they won't let anyone visit her.'

But he had to go. He had to go for Kashish. 'Ammi, I have to go for Kashish,' he said urgently. 'Please tell me which hospital.'

45

It felt like Kashish's ears hadn't stopped ringing. Ever since she saw Kinza at the foot of the stairs, bleeding, she had started screaming, and in her head, she was still screaming, even though she sat like a zombie outside the ICU while Kaif Bhai waited to speak to the doctor.

She was in shock. She still couldn't process what had happened in the space of a few seconds. One moment they had been shouting at each other, and the next, Kinza was in hospital. It seemed like some form of cosmic joke.

Allah couldn't be that cruel, could He?

Why not? Maybe He's punishing you. Because you deserve it. You caused the accident after all.

She covered her face with her hands and sobbed silently, her shoulders shaking. She tried to bring herself under control. She would break down later, when Kinza Api was out of danger. Until then, she couldn't afford to let go. Her stomach twisted and twisted until she was sure it had become a pretzel.

She curled her arm around her middle and rocked back and forth, muttering all the duas she knew, begging with

Allah to save her sister. Kaif Bhai returned, his face white. He sat down on the bench beside her and she was afraid to ask him what the doctors had said that had him looking so shocked, so haggard.

She couldn't bear to look at him. In her mind she played the scene over and over—how he came running and saw what had happened to Kinza. The way he had started crying, muttering 'no, no, no'. The kids were screaming.

Kashish had called the ambulance with heaving, shaky breaths, but Kaif Bhai couldn't wait for it to come. She didn't know if it was a good idea to move her, but she could see that waiting was making him go wild with fear.

She looked at her palm now, crusted with blood. Her sister's blood as she had cupped her head gently as Kaif Bhai carried her out. She had sat in the back of the car, holding her sister's head in her lap as Kaif Bhai drove. She hadn't given a single thought to where the kids were and she wondered if he had left them with the neighbours or they were alone at home. But she worried about them now.

'Where are the children?' she asked in a hoarse voice, still not looking at him.

'My sister is with them,' he said. 'I called her to come to the house. My family is on their way here.'

Kashish felt a crowding in her chest. She needed to know that Api was fine. That she was going to be all right. But she was scared to ask him, deathly afraid of voicing her fears.

'H-how is she?' she asked.

Kaif Bhai swallowed thickly. His eyes flooded with tears. 'They're not saying much, except that she's in a coma right now. They had to induce it to reduce the pressure on her brain.'

Her hand flew up to her mouth in shock.

'What?'

He nodded bitterly, tears falling down his cheeks. 'It's all my fault,' he whispered. 'My fault. I should have got that stair fixed. She kept telling me about it.'

Tell him. Tell him it's *your* fault.

But she couldn't open her mouth and admit it. She knew then he would want her to leave but there was no way she was leaving the hospital until Kinza was fine.

She would tell him later, when Api was home.

She couldn't think of the alternative. No. She just couldn't. Api couldn't die. She was too young! She had two kids who needed her, she had a husband who looked like he would die without her. She had…she had a sister who needed her too.

She covered her face and broke down, trying her best to control her crying. She had told herself she would cry later, but the tears kept falling, and her body shuddered. Kaif Bhai patted her back awkwardly, but she could sense that he was broken too.

'Can we see her?' she asked, when the tears were under control. She fished around for a tissue in the pocket of her jeans and wiped her nose with it.

'Only during ICU visiting hours,' Kaif Bhai said.

But she needed to see her. She had to apologise to Api for the horrible things she'd told her. How could she have been so awful to her? If Api hadn't been so angry at her, she would have looked where she was going. She wouldn't have slipped down the stairs.

They sat in strained silence until someone from Kaif Bhai's family came. It was his mother. She hugged him and started crying. Kashish got up from the bench uneasily and made place for her. Soon, Kaif Bhai was surrounded by his relatives, and she had never felt so starkly alone.

She wondered if Kaif Bhai had told Abbu. She should talk to Abbu and tell him, but then she remembered her phone was still in her bedroom. She hadn't brought it with her. Her fingers flexed. She stood at the window, her heart aching. It felt bruised and battered and she rubbed at her chest ineffectively.

'Kashish?'

She turned around at the voice, sure that she must have conjured it up. But no, there he was. Sameer stood at the end of the corridor, looking at her warily. She'd never been so glad to see someone, and nearly broke into a run as she walked towards him. Her steps grew quicker, until she was close to him. Then she launched herself at him, and he caught her, wrapping his arms around her.

She knew they were making a scene and a nurse glared as she walked past them. He had lifted her off her feet as he hugged her and she held on to him, as though she would collapse into tiny little pieces without his arm around her.

Finally, he set her down. She wiped her face but the tears kept coming. The people around Kaif Bhai, his relatives, were looking at her strangely. She didn't care.

'What happened?' he asked finally. She looked up at his earnest face and wanted to tell him everything. How it was her fault, that she was the worst sister on the planet. She didn't deserve any happiness. She didn't deserve anything. Maybe he saw some of it flash on her face, because he shook his head.

Still holding his hand, she dragged him away to an empty bench. There was enough space between them for another person to sit, and she was wary of closing the distance. Once he learned the truth about her, he wouldn't want to be anywhere near her. She should tell him everything. He deserved to know what an awful person she was.

To her surprise, he inched closer and picked up her hand. 'Kashish, it's okay. Take a deep breath.'

She realised just then that her breath had become choppy at the thought of coming clean to him. She took a deep breath. It didn't work.

'Come on, in and out,' he instructed softly. She wanted to yell at him. She didn't want his kindness. She didn't need him telling her what to do. But she listened to him, anyway. When she was relatively calm, she couldn't hold it in any longer.

Kaif Bhai was talking to his relatives, explaining something to his mother. He was pacing the corridor, mussing his hair up until it stood on end. His voice broke and he collapsed on the floor and someone helped him sit up.

Kashish and Sameer watched this unfold in horrified silence. She cleared her throat.

'This is all my fault.'

46

Sameer could hardly comprehend the garbled words Kashish was saying because every few seconds, she said, 'It was my fault.'

He put his hand on hers and squeezed tightly. 'Come on. Please. You didn't push her down the stairs. So how is it your fault?' he asked. He wanted to do whatever he could to help her, but he didn't know how.

She shook her head. 'You don't know, Sameer. We had a big fight,' she whispered. She clasped her throat, as if she was choking herself and he didn't stop to think as he reached up and pulled her hand down.

'Stop it. What are you doing?'

'I can't breathe.'

'Choking yourself will only make it worse.'

She swallowed and took deep breaths but it looked like she was trapped in her body and was frantically trying to escape.

'Do you want to get out of here for a bit?' he asked finally.

She shook her head. 'I can't. I can't go when she's in the ICU. I have to be here.'

He nodded. He understood. If it was one of his family members in there, he wouldn't have left either. But she was so distressed and he didn't know how to help her.

'Kashish, please stop blaming yourself. Whatever had to happen, happened. You know you can't stop fate, right?' he said, not sure if these were the right words. He didn't know what the right words could possibly be to someone like her who had already faced so much loss in her life.

'But I brought it on,' she said in a tortured whisper. She sniffled. 'She told me she wanted Abbu to get married. That made me so mad and angry about everything. I said some horrible things to her. I even threw Aunty K in her face, saying I was glad I made those videos.'

Sameer winced but didn't say anything. He just held her hand and squeezed. She didn't seem to notice.

'She can't die, Sameer,' she said, hiccupping, holding her head in her hands.

'What are the doctors saying?' he asked, feeling helpless.

'Kaif Bhai said that they've induced a coma to reduce the pressure on her brain. I don't know whether that's good or bad and I'm scared to ask anyone.'

He pulled out his phone and googled 'medically induced comas' and saw the number of results. It was not looking good, but he picked out the one thing that offered a shred of hope. 'Look, it says here that a medically induced coma is to help the patient heal. It's not too different from when someone is given anaesthesia. It's just about the dosage. And see, they can bring them out of a medically induced coma. She'll be out of it once the doctors feel that her body has recovered enough.'

The words should have assuaged her but Kashish broke down into noisy tears and a nurse came up to them and suggested they leave. She looked up at the nurse angrily but Sameer intervened and said that they would leave soon.

The nurse walked away, her shoes making a soft clip clop sound on the floor. To his surprise, Kaif Bhai came up to her and Sameer stood up, giving space for him to sit.

'Kashish, stop crying beta,' he said, his voice wobbling. Kashish looked at him, and Sameer could read the pure agony in her face, because no matter what he said, she was going to keep blaming herself until her sister woke up and forgave her. Kaif Bhai hugged her awkwardly, patting her back. 'I know how important she is to you. You know she always considers you her baby? Even before Kainaat and Kabir?'

Poor Kaif Bhai didn't know that these were the wrong words to tell Kashish because she only cried harder. She pulled away from Kaif Bhai. Was she going to tell him everything now? Sameer knew she should tell him the truth, but not now. Not when he was still dealing with everything else.

'Kaif Bhai,' she said softly, her throat working as she licked her lips.

Sameer reached out between them and tugged her hand. 'Come, let's go to the cafeteria and get you some water to drink.'

She looked at him angrily but he shook his head subtly and mouthed, 'not now'. Defeat slumped her shoulders as she got up from there.

'Yes, you get her something to eat as well, Sameer. Thank you so much for coming here today,' Kaif Bhai said, his voice cracking.

'Why did you stop me?' she asked him as they walked towards the lift.

'Don't burden him with your guilt right now, Kashish. Not when he's already so broken,' he said.

She crowded into a corner of the lift and squeezed her eyes shut. He didn't know what to do, but was glad they were alone in the lift and he walked the two strides it took to reach her and pulled her close.

She resisted at first but she finally came to him, her arms around his neck, her face buried in his chest as she cried.

He had no experience in dealing with a crying girl, especially not someone who had faced such a loss. But he tried his best. When the lift stopped at the cafeteria, she pulled away from him.

It was hard to believe that just a few hours ago they had shot the videos. She refused to sit down at a table and stood by, while he bought a bottle of water. She took it from him and gulped down half.

'Should we take something for Kaif Bhai and the others?' he asked. She shrugged, her red-rimmed eyes distant and lost. He bought some bottles of iced coffee and together, they walked back to the lift.

She was silent this time, not engaging with him and he didn't know how he could help her snap out of it.

'Does your father know?' he asked.

'I don't know,' she said with a huge sigh. She looked down at her feet as the lift stopped and shook her head. 'I'm a terrible daughter, and a horrible sister. You should go, Sameer. Don't hang around here for me. I'm not worth it. Because I know I'll be an awful girlfriend, too.'

He reached out and took her hand. 'That's not true, Kashish.'

'What kind of daughter doesn't want her father to be happy? What kind of sister says mean things to her sister and causes her accident?' she asked sharply. 'I'm just a selfish girl who can't think of anyone but myself.'

The lift doors opened and they stepped out. 'Truly selfish people never acknowledge that they're selfish,' he said finally.

She looked at him askance, almost as if she wanted to pick a fight with him and tell him to go.

He lifted her chin with his index finger. 'Do your worst. I'm not going anywhere.'

47

She wanted to ask him why. She wanted to know what made him come to the hospital and seek her out. But she kept quiet as she watched him hand the bottles of iced coffee to Kaif Bhai's relatives. Kaif Bhai thanked Sameer, patting him on the shoulder. A nurse came up and said something to Kaif Bhai and he straightened up and looked at Kashish.

What happened? No. No. Please no. Api can't die, she screamed in her head.

'ICU visiting hours are starting. Come, Kashish,' he called out to her. 'Only two people are allowed. The two of us can go.'

Kashish froze on the spot. She wanted to see her sister and she didn't want to, at the same time. What would she tell her? Kinza was in a coma. How could she bear to see her lying on the hospital bed like that? What if she broke down inside and was unable to stop crying?

The surprising source of strength that was Sameer prodded her from behind. 'Go,' he whispered. 'Go and talk to her.' Kaif Bhai had already gone inside and she would have to wait till he came outside.

Pursing her lips, she walked towards the ICU doors and waited. Sameer stood by her side, and unobtrusively slipped his hand into hers. She didn't know why he was here. She didn't know what he expected from her. But she knew she was glad that he had come. That she had meant enough to him to leave everything and come to the hospital to offer her support. She squeezed his hand back and he looked at her sideways.

'She'll be fine,' he said.

She shook her head. 'Don't give me those platitudes.'

He shrugged. 'They're not platitudes. I know it sounds like that but think of the positives. You guys brought her to one of the best hospitals in the city. She's being treated. And I'm sure the coma can be reversed the moment she's better. She'll be up and about in no time.'

How she desperately wanted to believe him. How she desperately needed the words to be true. She saw Kaif Bhai return and she let go of Sameer's hand.

Kaif Bhai looked pale and shaken and Kashish almost didn't want to go inside but she didn't stop to ask him how Api was doing. Two more doors and a few winding corridors later, she reached a large hall where all the ICU patients were kept. It was surprisingly loud in here. The tapping of shoes as nurses walked from patient to patient, the insistent beeping of machines, the steady tick tock of a clock on the wall, the very air seemed sucked of life.

She shuddered as she looked around for Kinza. Her gaze slid back to the end of the hall, where Kinza lay so lifeless, so silent, it was hard to believe they'd been shouting at each other just moments before this happened.

She walked up and stood near her. It felt odd talking to someone who couldn't talk back, but she couldn't just think her thoughts and hope Kinza would hear them. Anyhow, she wasn't going to hear them.

She tried to speak but the words got stuck in her throat. She cleared her throat softly, and looked around, hoping no one would come and tell her to leave. Breaths coming in short pants, she licked her lips and finally, tried to speak. 'Api, I'm sorry. Please, please forgive me. I didn't mean anything that I said. Please don't go away. I need you. Everyone needs you. You have to fight this and come back to us.'

Tears filled her eyes and her vision became blurry. Her sister, lying on the hospital bed, already looked like she wasn't of this world any longer. She moved closer, wary of touching her.

'Please, Api. Please get well so you can yell at me. You can tell me all the ways I'm a horrible sister,' she sniffed.

She felt a presence by her side and looked hurriedly. It was a nurse. 'Your sister?' she asked. Kashish nodded. She hoped the nurse would offer her comfort and tell her that Kinza was going to be fine but she didn't. She just nodded and walked away. She needed someone to tell her that her sister was going to emerge out of this, alive and well, but no one seemed inclined to tell that.

She stood there for a little longer, her eyes taking in the pale face of her sister who seemed impossibly small and shrunken on the bed. Every time she shut her eyes, she saw Kinza lying at the foot of the stairs. When she could no longer bear to see her sister lying so quietly, without offering her trademark saucy suggestions and remarks, she walked away. But at the door to the ICU, she turned back to look at her.

'Come back,' she whispered raggedly. 'Please. We need you. You're everything to us.'

Then she was outside and her eyes sought out Sameer who was sitting with Kaif Bhai. Kaif Bhai looked like he'd been rendered hollow, like any moment he was going to collapse in on himself. Sameer was talking to him softly, probably telling him how medically induced comas were reversible.

She felt a surge of emotion inside her, growing by the second as she neared them. Most of Kaif Bhai's relatives had left, barring his mother who sat on the uncomfortable bench stoically. But she couldn't look away from Sameer. He sensed her gaze and he looked up at her. He was trying to tell her not to say anything about the fight.

Not now, at least.

She gave an imperceptible nod and sat down beside Kaif Bhai. He was going to hate her when she told him what had led to Api's accident. She was never going to be welcome in their house again.

'Kashish, you should go home with Ammi. The kids must be scared. Go and talk to them. I'll be here,' Kaif Bhai said.

She shook her head. 'No, I'll stay here. You should go home and talk to them. They need to see you. You're their father. Go and comfort them. I'll be here,' she promised.

Kaif Bhai shook his head. 'I can't go. I can't leave her in the ICU and go,' he said thickly, his voice cracking.

'I'm not going either,' Kashish said firmly. 'And we need to tell Abbu and…'

'He's already on his way,' Kaif Bhai interrupted. 'But Kashish, someone needs to go home and…'

'Bhai, you take your mother and go home. I'll be here with Kashish. You can come back after some time and we'll all stay here,' Sameer said.

Kashish looked at him disbelievingly. Why would he stay here, waiting outside the ICU? Kinza was no one to him. But that wasn't true. Kinza was very important to her. And she was important to him. She could see it in his eyes.

48

'There's blood on your hands.'

Kashish gave him a strange look. 'Are you actually rubbing it in now?'

'Shit. I mean, there's literally blood on your hands,' Sameer said, slapping his forehead. 'You should wash it off.'

Kashish stared at her hands and shuddered. 'This is Kinza Api's blood,' she said faintly.

'I know. But you should wash it off, and come with me to the cafeteria so you can eat something.'

'Why are you so bossy?' she snapped at him, but she got up anyway and went to the restroom.

Kaif Bhai had left with his mother half an hour ago, promising to return as soon as he'd spoken to the kids. Kashish told him to take his time. She looked ready to sit outside the ICU for the rest of her life as penance.

Sameer was shocked at how strongly she felt about this being her fault and he really hoped that Kinza would get well and tell her that it was all right. Hopefully, she would forgive herself one day.

He texted Sadeem and updated him about the situation. His mother called him after a few moments, after Sadeem had relayed everything to her presumably.

'But why are you staying there?' she asked. 'I mean, I understand you wanted to comfort the poor girl but...'

'Ammi, I have to be here for her. I can't leave her and come,' he said. He saw the lift doors open. Kashish was back. There was no restroom on this floor.

'But what about college tomorrow and you can't possibly spend the night outside the ICU?'

His gaze was on Kashish as she walked towards him.

'She's very important to me, Ammi,' he said.

'I see,' Ammi said after a longish pause.

'I have to go now,' he said and ended the call. Kashish rejoined him on the bench and they sat in silence.

'Do you want to talk about it?' he asked.

She moved closer to him and put her head on his shoulders and his heart swelled. 'I already told you everything. There's nothing else to say. I was horrible to her. I was planning to leave tomorrow morning but then this happened.'

His heart shrank. She was going to leave tomorrow morning after the fight without even telling him? What about them? Wouldn't she have called him and told him about going back to Bangalore? She sensed the stiffness in his demeanour and lifted her head.

'I was thinking about us just before all this happened.'

'What about us?' he asked cautiously.

'I was thinking how different your family is compared to mine.'

He sighed and picked up her hand absently. 'Everyone's family is different, Kashish. And you should remember that no one's is perfect.'

She was silent for a moment. 'Mine was. When my mother was alive.'

He turned to her slightly. 'You were a child then. What you remember from back then may not be the truth of how things were.'

She growled softly and punched his bicep.

'Ouch. What was that for?'

'Stop being so sensible and all-knowing. You're annoying me.' But the words were said without any heat. He couldn't help himself, as he framed her face between his palms.

'I wish I was really all-knowing,' he said.

'Why?'

'I would have known what you were really thinking about us.'

She tugged her face away from him and looked away. 'You deserve someone nicer than me, Sameer,' she said quietly. 'I made a name by making fun of my sister who has been nothing but a mother to me. I was rude and so entitled. I expected her to make me her priority, and when her priorities changed after marriage, I was so angry with her. I'm not a good person.'

He stared at her in silence. 'I understand how you feel and the need to blame yourself, but...'

'Put yourself in my situation. Just for a moment,' she interrupted him.

He pursed his lips and even the thought of anything happening to Sadeem brought sweat to his forehead.

'See?' she whispered, shaking her head. She seemed to be coming to some sort of understanding with herself. 'You should go. We should end this before we're in any deeper. I don't want to ruin your life. Get away from me before it's too late.'

'You have an extremely high opinion of yourself,' he remarked.

She looked at him disbelievingly. 'What?'

'My life would be *ruined*? Please.' He snorted.

'I'm serious, Sameer.'

'I'm serious, too. In fact, I've never been more serious about anything else. And for the record, I'm already in too deep.'

They stared at each other for long moments and Sameer's heart was beating like a drum. 'Don't push me away. Let me be here for you.'

Her mouth trembled. 'I'm scared for Api.'

He nodded. 'I'm scared too. But I'm also choosing to be hopeful.'

'What if she…what if she doesn't make it?' she asked in a harsh whisper. 'Thanks to me, my niece and nephew will become motherless like me.'

He shook his head. 'Stop thinking about all that. Just have hope and faith. And pray for her.'

Nodding, she leaned against the wall and shut her eyes. He observed her face for a few moments. She did not look like Kashish Asif from her Instagram page, all polished and perfect. She looked like a normal teenager going through a very shitty day.

49

'Kashish.'

She woke up with a start. The waiting area outside the ICU was dark now, save for a tube light at one end. Many others were stretched out on the benches, sleeping. She looked up to see who had called out to her.

'Abbu,' she whispered and flung herself into his arms. She didn't know if there were any more tears left in her body but she sobbed as she held on to her father. He was here.

'Shh, it's going to be fine,' Abbu promised her, patting her back.

'You don't know that,' she hiccupped softly. She was hyper aware of the relative quietness of the hospital floor. The security guard outside the ICU was asleep. She looked around and saw that Sameer was also asleep, his back against the wall. Kaif Bhai was awake and he walked up to Abbu and hugged him quietly.

Abbu patted his back and sniffled. 'What happened?' he asked.

Sameer woke up just then and blinked. Then he sat up straighter and stood up. Abbu looked at him, confused, but he turned back to Kaif Bhai whose mouth trembled.

'There's a slippery spot on one of the top most stairs. She'd been asking me to get it fixed but I kept putting it off. She slipped from there and fell and it's all my fault,' he broke down as he finished talking.

Kashish couldn't help herself. She was going to come clean now.

'No, it's my fault, Kaif Bhai. Please stop blaming yourself. Api and I were fighting and she was angry with me. She didn't look where she was going because of me. *I'm* the one at fault here.' She realised Sameer was standing beside her, holding one of her hands.

Kaif Bhai stared at her. He was going to yell at her and tell her to never grace their home again. But there was no way she could let him keep thinking that he caused Api's accident.

'I heard the fight from our bedroom,' he said.

What?

Seeing her stunned expression, he spoke ruefully. 'She was upset about some videos you'd posted and told me about it when you were out. I told her not to take all of it so seriously. She'd been planning to talk to you and I told her it wasn't a good idea.' He glanced at Abbu but then looked back at her. 'Your reaction was expected, Kashish. Please don't blame yourself.'

Kashish felt like she'd been frozen. She shook herself out of her stupor. 'She fell because of me,' Kashish repeated.

'She fell because I didn't fix the stairs,' Kaif Bhai insisted. Abbu looked at her and then at Kaif Bhai.

'We'll share the blame later. But someone tell me how she is,' he said. Kashish was still shocked as she sat down on the bench while Kaif Bhai updated Abbu about Api's situation.

She had been expecting Sameer to leave but he said he was fine with staying by her side. She was glad he was there. She couldn't have faced this alone. When the duty doctor was just finishing his rounds, Kaif Bhai had walked up to him and asked him how Api was doing.

She was showing a little improvement but they were going to wait and see, the doctor informed them. Kaif Bhai kept telling her to go home with Sameer but she refused to leave. So the three of them had settled on the bench outside to wait.

Now, Kashish seemed to realise how late it was. 'You should go home. It's very late, Sameer,' she said. She was exhausted, too. But she couldn't, wouldn't go home. Not yet.

'I'm staying,' he said.

Although she was touched at his decision, she was also a little annoyed. 'Why?'

He glanced at her as if to see if she'd really asked the question. And then he glanced once at Abbu and Kaif Bhai, as if to confirm if they were still there. Of course, they were.

'Because I told you that...'

'This is a *family* matter, and now that my father is here, you should leave.'

Okay, that came out all wrong. She saw the flash of hurt in his eyes and then he stepped back as if she'd physically pushed him away.

'Sure. I'll leave,' he said and walked away before she could stop him.

Thankfully, neither Abbu nor Kaif Bhai made any remarks but as she sat down, Kaif Bhai sighed. 'You should have asked him to drop you home, Kashish,' he said.

Kashish shook her head. 'I need to be here when Api is awake,' she said. 'I have to apologise to her.'

'That makes two of us,' he muttered.

'What were you two fighting about?' Abbu intervened.

Kashish's eyes met Kaif Bhai's. A silent message passed between them. She exhaled.

'Do either of you have Instagram on your phones?' she asked.

'Why? Where's your phone?' Abbu asked. 'I called you so many times, by the way.'

'It's at home.' She took Kaif Bhai's phone and opened Instagram on it, navigating to her own page from his.

'Home?' Abbu asked, puzzled. 'But isn't it surgically attached to your palm?'

'Ha ha,' she replied drolly. She looked up at Abbu and Kaif Bhai. 'Api got to know just this morning that she's the inspiration behind my Aunty K videos.'

'Your what?' Abbu asked.

Sighing, she tapped play on one of the videos. 'See for yourself.' It was amazing, that until now this had seemed like the biggest hurdle in her life. Like it had been some big secret she was keeping from her family and bringing it up with Kinza had scared her so much. Now she'd do anything to have her yell at her about how much fun she'd made of her.

As they sat there, in the darkened hallway, her heart ached for multiple reasons. One was certainly for Sameer and the brusque, thankless way she'd sent him on his way. The other was for Kinza who was in the ICU. Abbu and Kaif Bhai were watching all the Aunty K videos one by one, and to her extreme surprise, there was no judgment from Kaif Bhai. In fact, she even saw him smile and chuckling at one where she'd depicted Aunty K calling her husband from her mother's house and lamenting at how clueless and lost he seemed without her.

'How did you do this?' Abbu asked, blinking.

She shrugged, glad he hadn't asked 'why'.

'She wasn't angry with you about this, Kashish,' Kaif Bhai said, forgetting the silent pact they'd both made not to tell Abbu what Kashish and Kinza had really fought over.

'But she said she was hurt.'

'You've known your sister all your life, and you didn't know the most important thing about her?' Kaif Bhai asked. He sounded almost normal, almost as if he'd forgotten that the love of his life was inside the ICU.

'What?' she asked.

'She was hurt that you hadn't told her about it. That you hadn't let her join in on all the fun.'

Kashish shook her head. 'No way. Are you saying she would have joined in and not slapped me?'

Kaif Bhai nodded. 'What's that you kids call these days? FOMA? Your Api's FOMA is very strong.'

'FOMO, Kaif Bhai. FOMO,' she corrected him with a giggle.

'What is FOMA, FOMO?' Abbu asked, puzzled.

'Fear Of Missing Out,' Kashish explained, but Abbu wasn't listening. He was looking at one of the videos where Kashish was flinging back her braid dramatically, her hand on her hip.

'Amazing,' he muttered. 'It's like seeing a mirror image of your sister.'

Kashish bit down on her lower lip. 'I'll delete my account. I'll get rid of all the videos,' she said.

'What? Why?' Kaif Bhai asked, startled.

'I don't care about any of that. I just want her back.'

'And you will, beta,' Abbu said, patting her back. 'You will. But don't delete these. Your sister will kill you because of her FOMA, FOMO.'

'Well, she better come out of that coma soon then,' Kashish settled her back against the wall. Her lower back ached, and she wished there was some place she could just curl up and sleep. 'Because otherwise, imagine how much she'll be missing out on?'

Neither of them replied, and Kashish shut her eyes. This time, instead of Kinza, she saw Sameer, and on remembering the look of hurt in his eyes, she sighed.

So many bridges to mend.

50

'Let him sleep.'

'But he'll be late for college!'

'He's not going to college today.'

'How come you're so cool with him missing college and when I want to take leave…'

Silence.

'Ouch. You can't twist my ear! I'm seventeen now!'

'Will the two of you stop talking over my head?' Sameer grumbled, burying his head under the pillow. But Ammi and Sadeem ignored him.

'Let go of my ear, Ammi. I'm the good boy here, going to school while Romeo here was out with his girlfriend and you didn't say a word to him.'

At this, Sameer got up and scowled, the bed covers falling away. His hair was tousled and his eyes felt gritty and dry. He blinked as the people before him became clearer. Ammi stood with her arms folded across her chest formidably. Sadeem skulked in a corner, fiddling with his school bag.

'I thought you weren't coming back last night?' Ammi asked.

He didn't want to be reminded of the casual way Kashish had flicked him away, like he'd been an annoying pest.

'Her father came so I knew she had someone with her. So I left,' Sameer said. Ammi looked at him shrewdly.

'How's Kinza?'

'I don't know. I have to find out,' he said, getting up from the bed and wincing as pins and needles shot through his back. He'd reached home at 3 a.m. and fallen into bed directly, trying not to think about how much he was hurting over Kashish's dismissal of him.

'I'm getting late for school. Are you giving me breakfast or not?' Sadeem scowled. Ammi shook her head and walked out, then she leaned back into the room.

'We need to talk,' she said and she walked away.

Sameer groaned. He wasn't in any mood to talk to his mother or anyone for that matter. He just wanted to lie in bed and not think about anything. He pulled out his phone and texted Kashish, asking her if there were any updates on Kinza, but the tick remained single.

Frowning, he put away his phone and went to the bathroom to shower. When he had changed into fresh clothes, Ammi returned.

'You're going to college?' she asked.

'I thought I could still make it even though I'll miss the first class,' he replied, surprised that Ammi didn't expect him to go.

'But don't you want to go to the hospital and check in on Kinza? And Kashish?' Ammi asked.

Sameer looked at his mother warily. Where was she going with this? Was she implying that she was okay with him seeing Kashish? He scratched the back of his neck awkwardly. He didn't have the sort of relationship with his mother where he could tell her about his crushes and all that.

And overall this was quite embarrassing. But his mother wouldn't let it go.

'Aren't you getting late for work?' he asked, trying to buy a little more time for himself.

She shook her head. 'What happened? Tell me.'

'Nothing happened, Ammi. She was very upset about her sister being in the hospital,' he explained. Ammi nodded. 'Then, her brother-in-law kept asking me to go home but I knew she wanted me there. I could sense she was feeling alone.'

'And she sent you packing the moment her father came?' Ammi asked sharply.

Sameer nodded. He felt like shit when he thought of how she had enunciated that it was a 'family' matter.

'I don't know her reasons for sending you away, Sameer,' Ammi said. 'But you told me she was important to you. So why didn't you fight to stay?'

He was surprised at the question, but he shrugged. 'I don't know. I felt unwanted there so I came away.'

'She's a fool if she can't see you for the gem you are,' Ammi said, impassioned.

'Ammi, please,' he said, embarrassed but mildly pleased. Ammi should have praised him before Sadeem though. He'd have eternal bragging rights.

'Listen, I just wanted to tell you to take it easy today. Don't go to college if you're tired. You barely slept.' Ammi made to go and Sameer stopped her.

'So you're okay with me seeing Kashish?' he blurted out.

Ammi's eyebrows went up. 'Well, when you put it like that…' she muttered, then she sighed. 'I don't mind, Sameer. But looks like she's the one you'll have to convince.'

That much was true, Sameer thought ruefully, as Ammi walked away. He wondered what Kashish was doing, and why she hadn't replied to his text. That was when he remembered that she didn't have her phone with her.

Uneasily, he dialled Kaif Bhai's number that he had taken last night. How had Kinza fared during the night? He really hoped for all their sakes that she had improved and would become better. When the phone kept ringing and ringing, Sameer became uneasy. He felt a trickle of sweat running down his spine.

All kinds of horrible thoughts flowed through his mind. He stood up, decision made. Kashish had asked him to leave but it was a new day and he wasn't going to leave, not until he knew for certain that Kinza was fine. That Kashish was fine.

Ammi was still at home when he left, telling her he was going to the hospital.

'Keep us updated,' she called out as he got onto his motorcycle and rode to the hospital. His thoughts were all jumbled in his head. Ammi was right. Last night he should have stayed back. He'd have known what was happening in the hospital right now. Instead, he'd been affronted at what Kashish implied and he'd come home.

What if the worst had happened, he wondered. His heart broke for Kashish. She would be devastated and he couldn't even begin to imagine Kaif Bhai's state. No, please no. That can't happen. Kinza's was a life-threatening injury. That was why she was in the medically induced coma.

He reached the hospital, parked the motorcycle in the basement parking and hurried towards the lift. His legs felt like rubber as he thought of all that could have gone wrong while he slept at home on his comfortable bed and sulked about Kashish giving him the boot. Why had he come away? Because of self-respect? Yeah sure, but what did that matter now?

He reached the ICU floor, his eyes seeking out Kashish and Kaif Bhai and Kashish's father. But all three of them were conspicuous by their absence.

51

Half an hour before Sameer turned up at the hospital, Kashish had just returned from the restroom after washing her face. She didn't want to leave. She felt scared, in a superstitious sort of way, that if she left, something would happen to Kinza. And if it hadn't been a pressing need to pee, she wouldn't have left her spot outside the ICU at all.

Poor Abbu looked uncomfortable, but he and Kaif Bhai were both dozing, and she let them sleep. She still couldn't believe how blasé they had both been about the Instagram thing. And here she'd been getting all worked up about how they would react. Abbu was actually embarrassed that he lived with Kashish and had never realised what an excellent mimic and actress she was. That she made all these videos and he'd never once noticed or seen her at it.

Kashish had been serious about shutting it all down. Having a million followers meant nothing if her sister wasn't with her. She needed Kinza to get through this. She spotted one of the duty doctors going inside the ICU for their rounds and her heart leapt.

To her surprise, the duty doctor emerged not even a few moments later and came straight towards them. Kashish stood up, the action waking up both Abbu and Kaif Bhai. They all stood up, and Kashish felt like her hair had just been electrified. The doctor's face was covered with a face mask and there was no way of gauging her expression.

Something was wrong. That was why she was coming outside to talk to them. Her heart sank to her feet and she didn't know how she was going to bear it. What would this do to Kaif Bhai and the kids? How she had resented them all for taking away Kinza Api, and now, thanks to their fight, she was taking her away from them, forever.

This can't be happening.

The duty doctor stood before them. Kashish dreaded the moment the doctor would open her mouth and speak to them. Her stomach clenched painfully.

'She's awake and she wants to see someone from her family,' the doctor said.

For a second or so, no one moved. Then Abbu and Kashish looked at each other, eyes wide while Kaif Bhai ran into the ICU, his face joyous, even as he laughed and cried at the same time.

'How?' Kashish asked the duty doctor, but the truth was, she didn't care how. She was just glad her sister was awake.

'Yesterday, the doctor changed her dosage during his last rounds,' the duty doctor said. 'I don't know why he did that.' She shrugged.

'So she's awake now? We can all see her?'

‘Normally, I’d tell you all to wait till ICU visiting hours, but she’s insisting on meeting someone from her family,’ the doctor said.

‘I want to see her,’ Kashish blurted out before she could stop herself. But the duty doctor shook her head.

‘Patients are all sleeping at this time. I only came out to call you because she was getting a little agitated, insisting on seeing someone.’

Just then, Kaif Bhai came out, his face all lit up. He ran to them and put his hands on her shoulders. ‘One of you go and talk to her. I need to speak to the admin department and arrange for her to be shifted to a regular room.’

The doctor shook her head vehemently, but Kashish gave her a pleading look. ‘Please? I won’t take long. Promise.’

‘Just five minutes,’ the doctor relented.

Kashish looked at Abbu, torn because she knew he’d want to go and see her too. She was his daughter after all.

Abbu patted her arm. ‘You go on. I’ll go with Kaif and see if he needs any help.’

Wiping her eyes, Kashish nearly ran into the ICU, unable to believe that this had really happened. She put her hand in her pocket to pull out her phone and tell Sameer and then remembered she still didn’t have her phone.

She cursed herself for her stupidity in sending him away. What on earth had gotten into her? She’d just been embarrassed at facing Abbu with him, even though Sameer’s earnestness was evident for all to see. Now, he was the first person she wanted to talk to after getting this news that Kinza was out of her coma.

All thoughts of cute boys flew out of her head as she walked into the ICU. A little corner of her mind told her not to rejoice just yet. The doctor hadn't said that she was out of danger or anything. But why else would Kaif Bhai need to speak about arranging a regular room?

Finally, she was before her.

Kinza was staring at the ceiling. She looked at Kashish and blinked a couple of times.

'Api,' Kashish whispered. Her heart was pounding loudly. What should she tell her? She didn't want to waste even a single second, but the words were all jumbled up in her brain.

Should she apologise first? Should she beg for her forgiveness? She was sure she'd end up making a scene with all her crying (she was still capable of crying surprisingly, even though she had thought she was all out of tears last night) and then she'd get kicked out of the ICU right away.

'Api,' she said again as she moved closer.

'Can you…' Kinza said, her voice coming out as a croak.

Kashish looked around, hoping to spot some nurse or doctor. Did Api need water? She looked up at the monitors above and speed read everything although it made no sense to her.

'What do you want?' she asked, unable to stop herself from reaching out and holding Kinza's hand. Kinza squeezed her hand back, weakly.

Licking her lips, Kashish spoke rapidly. 'Before anything else, I just want to tell you how sorry I am for all the things I said to you.'

Kinza shut her eyes once and then opened them. 'Forget that,' she rasped.

'Never! I said horrible things to you and I know you only had everyone's best interests at heart.'

'I said…forget that,' she insisted.

'But…'

'If I had died now and Kaif got married again, I would have been very, very mad,' Kinza said slowly.

'Don't say such things!' Kashish nearly cried out in horror.

Kinza winced. 'Stop shouting! My brain is still hurting.'

'Sorry! Sorry!'

'I would have come back to haunt him if he'd done that.'

'But you said it's been so many years since Ammi…'

'*Forget* I said that. It's Abbu's choice. His wish,' she said.

Kashish nodded.

'Again, I'm very sorry Api and…'

'Can you help me?'

'Anything. What do you want?' Kashish asked her eagerly, ready to do whatever it took.

'Can you help me set up my Instagram account?'

52

Kashish stared at her sister. Was she serious?

Kinza sighed. 'Must be the drugs talking,' she muttered. At this, Kashish let out a burble of laughter that she quickly controlled before a disapproving nurse kicked her out.

Kinza looked around. 'God, I'm so bored already. When are they letting me out of here?'

Kashish rolled her eyes. 'You had a life-threatening injury and the doctors had to induce a coma. They're hopefully not letting you out any time soon.'

Kinza pouted and then grimaced. 'I should have stayed in the coma only then. Who woke me up?'

Kashish shook her head, amazed at how calm Kinza seemed. She moved closer to her sister, aware that she'd need to leave soon. Any moment, a brisk-stepping nurse was going to kick her out.

'Listen, Api. I mean it. I'm a terrible sister. And I'm really sorry about all the horrible things I told you,' she said quietly.

Kinza's face softened. 'It happens, Munni. It's okay. Ammi and I used to have big fights too.' Kashish frowned.

'What? When?'

'Well, some happened before you were born,' she said sardonically, and then she yawned. She looked tired.

'I'll leave?' Kashish asked.

'No, stay. Stay until they send you out,' Kinza said.

Kashish didn't know what to say to her, so she stood by her side awkwardly, while Kinza looked around. Then she heard a nurse walking towards her and knew it was time to leave.

'Listen,' Kinza said.

'Yeah?'

'When you're making videos about Aunty K getting hospitalised, then you better use me,' she said. 'Pretty sure I can act better than you.'

Kashish was glad the nurse asked her to leave because she had no idea what to tell her sister. That was how she emerged from the ICU, her face wreathed in a smile. Then she walked right into Sameer who was hovering outside the door anxiously.

'Sameer!' she stood back to see him clearly. He looked worried but her heart swelled with some unidentifiable emotion on seeing him.

'Hey! Everything okay? Where's your father and Kaif Bhai? How's Kinza?' he asked. 'What were you doing inside so early in the day?'

'She's awake!' Kashish said, a huge smile on her face. After yesterday, it had seemed impossible that she could smile at all.

'What? That's amazing!' He looked shocked but also happy.

'I know!'

And then, she didn't think at all. She just stepped forward and hugged him. If he was surprised, he didn't show it but wrapped his arms around her and hugged her back. She was going to apologise to him about how she'd behaved last night when someone cleared their throat. Kashish stepped away from Sameer, her embarrassment turning into shock when she saw that it was Abbu and Kaif Bhai.

'I…er…um…' she stalled, not sure what to tell anyone. Instead of getting embarrassed himself, Sameer picked up her hand and held it. She didn't pull away. Abbu lifted an eyebrow.

'We didn't meet properly last night,' Abbu addressed Sameer.

'Sameer Ehsan,' Sameer said, putting out one hand to shake Abbu's. Abbu looked at it for a moment before taking his hand.

'But who are you? Why are you here?' Abbu asked, his chest puffing up a little.

Sameer turned to her. Things between them were still undefined.

Wincing a little, Kashish took a deep breath. If Abbu had asked her before Kinza's accident, she may have told him that Sameer was a fellow Instagrammer and they were collaborating on some videos. But now, everything had changed.

'He's my boyfriend,' she said nervously. Abbu's eyes widened in shock and his mouth fell open. But before he could say anything, she spoke up quickly. 'Abbu please. Not now. We'll talk about this later.'

Kaif Bhai thankfully intervened. 'You should go home, Kashish. Take a nap maybe? And freshen up a little and come back. By then she'll hopefully be shifted to a room.'

Kashish stared at him in horror. *Freshen up*. God, she was probably a mess! She needed a shower. She needed to change her clothes. Some of Kinza's blood was still on her top. And she'd hugged Sameer like this. Sameer who looked as fresh as a daisy. She tried to move away from him but he wouldn't let her. He held her hand and gave her a funny look.

'I can take you home,' he said in a low voice. Kashish looked at Abbu. His nostrils were flaring in a way she'd hardly ever seen before.

'Whose home?' he asked, almost belligerently.

'Kinza Api's obviously,' Kashish said, trying to sound nonchalant. She was relieved when Kaif Bhai patted Abbu's back and spoke softly to him, and probably told him that he trusted Sameer.

Abbu's face changed only marginally.

'I'm going to see if they'll let me see Kinza,' he said and he walked into the ICU.

She finally looked at Sameer, aware that she hadn't looked at him since she'd introduced him as her boyfriend to her father. There was a look of amusement in his eyes, paired with a bit of anxiety, but through it all, he hadn't let go of her hand.

53

The sun was already up in the sky and it was beating down on them ferociously as Sameer rode his motorcycle towards Kinza's home. His mind kept wanting to replay all the moments from this morning, but he couldn't, not just yet.

He was her boyfriend.

That thought brought a smile to his face and an increased awareness of Kashish sitting behind him. They needed to talk but she probably wanted to rest a bit first.

'Can you stop somewhere for a bit?' she asked him. Surprised, he slowed the motorcycle and brought it to a stop in a by-lane.

'What happened?' he asked as she hopped down. She looked nervous.

'I realised I wouldn't be able to talk to you once we get home,' she said. She looked exhausted but there was that same underlying beauty he'd always noticed about her.

He nodded. 'Go ahead.'

'First of all, I'm sorry about asking you to leave last night.'

There was some unidentifiable emotion in the depths of her eyes.

'I don't have any excuse, I guess. I just felt like I'd already put you through so much trouble and Abbu was there and he would wonder who you were and I just couldn't deal with it then,' she said.

He nodded. Like she said, it was no excuse but at least she was being honest.

'I was hurt,' he admitted. She looked contrite. 'But it's okay. I wasn't sure I'd be welcome in the hospital this morning but I called Kaif Bhai to ask how Kinza was doing and he didn't answer. That made me panic and I came right away.'

'He was probably inside the ICU then, I think. Or maybe his phone charge ran out. He's been fielding calls from so many people since yesterday,' Kashish explained.

'I just got so worried.'

She nodded. 'I know. This morning when the duty doctor came to us, I had all sorts of horrible thoughts going through my head. And my sister…' she trailed off, with a giggle.

'What?'

'You won't believe what she asked me.'

'What did she ask you?' he asked, smiling because he couldn't help himself in the face of her evident happiness.

'She wants me to help her set up her Instagram. And she said if I made an Aunty K video about her being in the hospital, she wanted to act in it.'

Sameer's mouth dropped open in shocked surprise. 'What?'

'I know, right? She said it must be all the drugs talking and I suspect she may not be so ready to forgive me once she's back home.'

'Well, I'm glad things got resolved between the two of you,' he said finally.

'And between us,' she admitted.

'So I guess I'm your boyfriend then?'

She nodded. 'If you still want to be. Obviously, I can be very high maintenance and I'm a bit of a diva and I…'

He pulled her towards him and she squeaked out a surprised, 'What?'

'My diva girlfriend doesn't babble,' he said, bending down to kiss her. She kissed him back enthusiastically, until a traffic cop screeched to a stop beside them.

'Uh oh,' she murmured as she stepped away from him. 'Are we in trouble?'

'Depends. How ready are you to see some spectacularly bad acting?' Sameer asked as he walked towards the traffic cop.

'I'm going to record it for posterity,' she said. He rolled his eyes.

'But I don't have my phone!' she wailed. Turning around, he tossed his phone to her and she caught it expertly.

Half an hour later, five hundred rupees lighter, they finally reached Kinza's home.

'You have to explain what actually happened,' she said as she got down from the motorcycle. The entire conversation with the cop had been in Tamil and although she'd recorded it unobtrusively, Kashish had no idea what had actually transpired.

'I explained to him that I was taking you to the hospital and you were complaining of breathing problems so I was giving you mouth-to-mouth resuscitation.'

'And he bought that?' Kashish asked, wide-eyed.

Of course not. The actual conversation had been very different but Kashish wouldn't know, would she?

'We might need to practise some more,' he said solemnly. 'The cop was saying I was doing it all wrong.'

'You're pulling my leg,' she was grinning.

'But seriously, Kashish,' he said, reaching out to hold her hand. 'How is this going to work?'

She looked worried too, but she took a deep breath. 'We'll make it work, Sameer. One day at a time.'

Epilogue

One year later

'Are you always like this?'

'Like what?'

'This distracting?'

'I'm distracting you? I didn't know that.'

'Stop it. I'm getting everything wrong. And she'll overhear us.'

'Okay fine. But she's too excited to notice. She won't overhear us at all.'

'You don't know that for sure. She's got the ears of a hawk.'

'Um, Kashish, it's *eyes* of a hawk.'

'Bah. Fine. Ears of whatever has sharp ears.'

'Bats. Bats have excellent hearing.'

'Great. Now she'll think I'm calling her a bat. Just get this shot done.'

'Please is the magic word, your highness.'

'Ugh. Stop it, Sameer. Don't make me all…'

'Hot and bothered?'

'Shush. Let's finish this damn video first.'

'I told you I can handle being behind the camera. You should go and join her.'

'I don't know if this is such a good idea.'

'You convinced me to come all the way from Chennai for it.'

'That was just an excuse to get you here.'

'You know you don't need excuses, right? I'm *easy* where you're concerned.'

'She's really going to hear us and then she'll take me over her knee and spank me.'

'Why are you giving me all these ideas?'

'Oh my god. Just shoot the video! Why am I dating you?'

'You love me.'

'Only because my brain is also damaged.'

'Are you talking about my accident?'

'Shit. No, of course not, Kinza Api. Sameer and I were just discussing the video. Why would we talk about your accident?'

'I heard something about brain damage.'

'Thank god she didn't hear the part where you called me a horny asshole.'

'Should I come there? I'm thinking maybe we can add something to the script.'

'Oh no. No Api. The script is fine. We'll do a quick rehearsal and then we'll shoot for real.'

'Go now. I've got it under control.'

'Are you sure? Because we've never done this sort of thing before.'

'I think your audience is going to *love* seeing the inspiration behind Aunty K.'

'I can't believe she's making me do this.'

'Maybe I should change my outfit.'

'No Api! It's perfect! Don't change anything! I'm coming there.'

'Kashish Asif.'

'What?'

'Go and be your awesome self. This video will be perfect. Better than anything else you've done.'

'You think so?'

'I know so.'

'Okay, let's do this.'

'Oh my god, Sameer. That's not what I meant! She'll see us!'

'Well, we have her blessings, don't we?'

'You're crazy if you think you can get away with a kiss when she's in the same room.'

'Then I have to work on getting her out of the room as soon as I can. So you'd better hurry up and finish this video.'

'You're really crazy.'

'I don't disagree.'

Kashish shoved Sameer's chest playfully but blew him a kiss when she was sure Kinza wasn't looking. He pretended to catch it and hold it to his chest. Giggling, she walked over to her sister and the two of them sat down on the bed to record the planned video.

'Ready?'

'I don't know. What if everyone laughs at me?'

Kashish gave Kinza a look.

'Fine. Fine. I know that's the point. We want to make people laugh. Let's do this.'

Kashish looked at Sameer. In the past year, a lot had changed in both their lives. Sameer's career as an Instagrammer had picked up when the video they shot in his home with Kashish went viral and now he had a staggering 2.5 million followers. The audience had loved the story of how they got together and Kashish was now dealing with 10 million followers, not sure how she'd reached this stage.

Life was busy for the two of them, as they were shooting videos, and they were both earning fairly decently with paid collaborations and everything. But they still made it a point to shoot a few videos together, as a valid excuse to spend time with each other. She didn't know what they'd both do when they finished college but all that was for later. Anyhow, Ammajan insisted she wanted her own Instagram account, even though the only things she posted on it were photos of goats on the street outside her house in Vellore. She now had 10,000 followers and Sadeem liked to joke that she was the G.O.A.T.

Sameer hit the record button and gave a thumbs up sign. Kashish turned to Kinza. They were both dressed identically, in one of the typical Aunty K outfits.

'Is it true? That actually, *you're* Aunty K?'

Kinza looked petrified for the barest of moments, but then she straightened her back and channelled, um, wait, was that Sushmita Sen? Or Kareena Kapoor?

'*Of course, I'm Aunty K!*'

Each word was punctuated with an over-the-top movement of her head, so definitely Kareena Kapoor.

Kashish managed to get a quick look at Sameer before she got into character, and the merriment in his eyes, and the quiet shaking of his shoulders was enough indication that this video was going to be just perfect.

Acknowledgements

It's always a relief for me to get back to writing Young Adult fiction and firstly I have to thank my editor Sudeshna for gently encouraging me to come back to my first love. Thanks to the Speaking Tiger team of Dyuti and Anjali for reading the proofs. To Maithili for designing the cover. I also want to thank my friends and beta readers Shilpa Suraj and Apeksha Rao, who read *literally* everything I write. A huge thank you to my family who has always turned a blind eye to my writing frenzy, aware that some sort of magic is happening behind the office doors and they'll get to know soon. Of course, another big thank you to my faithful readers who constantly surprise me and overwhelm me with their love and their messages of support. Lastly, a thank you to Allah for keeping my mind running with ideas and my fingers flying over the keyboard.